nF419531

Abiding in the Secret Place

VOLUME 11

Prayer Points for Everyday Use

Nicole G. McLeary

Copyright © 2024-Nicole G. McLeary

All Rights Reserved
Abiding in the Secret Place Journal
Nicole G. McLeary

Except as provided by the Copyright Act of Jamaica (1993)
no part of this publication may be reproduced, stored in a
retrieval system or transmitted in any form or by any means
without the prior written permission of the publisher.

For additional copies of this book and other ministry
publications, services and offerings please contact the
author.
nicolemclearyministries@gmail.com

YouTube https://bit.ly/2VH3vyN

Facebook https://bit.ly/3qGq6d9

Instagram https://bit.ly/3lSN2SC

<u>**DEDICATION**</u>

The book is dedicated to the lady who taught me how to pray and who laid the foundation for me to become a second-generation prayer warrior. This is none other than my precious mother.

Thank you for all the ways you showed me the importance of prayer. I am grateful for all the family prayer meetings, intercessory meetings and best of all the Redemption Hymnal that we sang our prayer choruses from. You invested well and I am certain that God will continue to reward you richly in this life and in the life to come.

Abiding in the Secret Place

Testimonials

I first got a copy of this amazing prayer book – Abiding in The Secret Place in 2013 and used it in my training sessions with my colleagues. They also fell in love with it and as such I sold over (50) fifty copies within that year. I ensured every family member as well as my friends got a copy and we have been using it ever since. My testimonies are too numerous to name here, but the book has simply been a blessing to not just me but to my entire family. Grab a copy and use it! I promise it will structure your life, like it has done for me and countless others I know!
Nadine Isaacs-Brown- Entrepreneur, Financial Adviser & Motivational Speaker

*I appreciate this book very much. It propelled my drive for prayer and kept me on the right path. The Prayer Points have pushed me into another realm of prayer. Thank you so much Pastor Nicole McLeary for this game-changing book that has transformed my prayer life.- **Sashae Jackson- Intercessor***

Having a prayer book is integral for any individual. I wholeheartedly recommend Abiding in the Secret place written by Prophetess Nicole, just the name abiding says a lot. I use this prayer book in several sessions; at family devotions, all-night prayer meetings, at church and in my personal prayer time. I also recommend this book for church leaders as it is a good tool to develop your congregation in prayer. It is so ironic that when I got married my husband had one of these books in his collection and we lived miles away then. You need to get this book it is a great gift to share. I am happy to have and look forward to the next edition!
Angella Ricketts- Minister of Religion

<u>***Progress & Social Wellbeing***</u>

2.11 New Beginnings
2.12 Favour & Elevation
2.13 Abundant Living
2.14 Divine Connections
2.15 Destiny Helpers
2.16 Seasons of Promotion
2.17 Ease in Progress
2.18 The Blessing of a Thousand
2.19 Alignment with Purpose & Destiny

<u>***Financial Prosperity***</u>

2.20 Spirits of Poverty & Financial Drought
2.21 Financial Slavery & Hardship
2.22 Spirits of Lack
2.23 Financial Sabotage
2.24 Financial Deliverance & Breakthrough
2.25 The Realm of Prosperity
2.26 Building Generational Wealth

<u>***Physical Healing***</u>

2.27 Undiagnosed Sicknesses & Diseases
2.28 Seasonal Sicknesses
2.29 Genetic Weaknesses
2.30 Degenerative Diseases
2.31 Deformities & Paralysis
2.32 Healing & Creative Miracles

Introduction

The following programme is designed to rebuild the fundamental principle of prayer. The kind of prayer that is birth out of intimacy with God cannot be overly stressed. There is an urgent need in the body of Christ for just this. David said if the foundations are removed what will the righteous do (Ps11:3).

The word used here for foundation means prince, column or chief place. Prayer is one of the foundations of spiritual health. The same material that built the foundation of Jerusalem, is the same thing that built its walls. Nehemiah was heartbroken because the walls of Jerusalem were broken down (Neh. 1:3). The walls were a defence and a means of protection. When the walls came down the people were exposed and vulnerable to the elements that were without. Israel's enemies had complete access to ravish and ruin her.

God promised to build a wall of fire around His people (Zech 2:5) but this can only happen when we stir ourselves up to seek Him. The people who will build altars unto the Lord, are the ones who will see and experience fire (Genesis 15:17-18, 1 Kings 18: 31-38). We then will become handlers of fire, if we consistently bring a sacrifice to God. It's time for the walls of fire to be built around our lives, homes, communities, workplaces, nation and the nations of the world.

The time has come for prayer to dominate every aspect of our lives. The heavens are open; the pockets in the spirit realm are pregnant with unusual blessings and anointings. God is looking for fertile soil to deposit His treasure in. Someone in our generation needs to tap into the realm of the supernatural, in a way we have never seen before. Deep must call to deep in this season! (Psa. 42).

The weighty price must be paid to leave a legacy for the generation to come. The Bible says that a good father lays up wealth for two generations (Pro 13:22). The spiritual wealth that we are looking for can only be mined out of the spirit through prayer.

The ones that have been given access to the mysteries of the kingdom must be the ones who are ready to do the underground work of travail.

The pioneers in the spirit must emerge from out of the limitations of false religion. That which is and is to come is calling us to higher ground. These prayer points are designed to help you develop a consistent and powerful prayer life. Welcome to a course of action that will change your life and everything around you!

PART I

REPENTANCE & SANCTIFICATION

Active repentance is a part of a Christian's spiritual health. These prayer points are designed to help you maintain your spiritual purity and are an aid to consistently keep you in the presence of God.

1.1 Repentance & Spiritual Examination

Scriptural Prayer Aids: 2 Chronicles 6:36-39, Jeremiah 18:8, Joel 2:12- 13

Petition:

- Holy Father, I come to you in the name of Jesus Christ.

- God, I thank you, that it is your grace that leads me to repentance.

- Father, I am weak and my righteousness is as filthy rags so I fall on your mercy right now.

- To you O God do I lift up my soul, I ask that you cause your truth to become my reality.

- I lay all that I am and hope to become on the altar.

- Oh Lord, if you should count iniquity no one would be able to stand before you.

- I repent of all the things that I have thought, said and done that has misrepresented your kingdom.

- Heal me O God from my backslidings, turn me Father and I will be turned, change me and I will be transformed.

- According to your tender mercies blot out my transgressions and remember my sins no more, remove them from me, even as far as the east is from the west.

- Cleanse me Lord and quicken me, so that I may call upon your name.

- Father, awaken me out of slumber, and repair every breach that is in my life.

- Father of light, I ask that you shine your light into my dark places, in the name of Jesus.

- Examine my heart and remove everything that wars against your will.

- Oh Lord, unite my heart to fear you.

- Keep me from double-mindedness and spiritual instability.

- Let the words of my mouth and the meditation of my heart, be acceptable in your sight.

- Give me a heart that is completely sold out to you.

- Father, forgive me if I have drawn near to you with my lips and my heart is far from you.

- Lord, help me not to allow my heart to deceive me.

- Let your truth find place in my inward parts.

- Father, let no spirit of deception and falsehood rule over my life.

- Let the desires of my heart always line up with your will.

- Let the iniquity of my generation be purged from my heart, in the name of Jesus.

- Father, give me a tender and compassionate heart, one that is full of mercy and love.

- Father, cleanse my heart of selfishness and pride.

- God let envy, jealously and malice not be found in me.

- Merciful Father, create in me a clean heart and renew a right spirit within me.

- Give me a broken and a contrite heart O Lord.

- Help me to seek you with all of my heart.

- Let your words never slip from my heart in Jesus' name.

- Give me a heart that will fear you and keep your commandments.

- Lord, if my heart has strayed towards idols, I ask that you forgive me.

- Father give me a heart that truly longs after you.

- God, I thank you that my heart truly belongs to you and you will keep it from corruption. Amen.

1.2 Dying to the Flesh

Scriptural Prayer Aids: 1 Corinthians 15:31, Galatians 2:19-20, Colossians 3:5, Philippians 3:10-11
Petition:

- Father, I thank you for the sacrifice that Christ made on my behalf.

- I know that you require no less a sacrifice from me.

- So today, I lay down my life so I can gain spiritual life.

- Father, let every work of the flesh die in my life, in the name of Jesus.

- Father, help me not to make provision for the flesh.

- Cause me to forsake the youthful lusts that war against the soul.

- Help me to flee fornication in the name of Jesus.

- Help me to kill the deeds of the flesh in the name of Jesus.

- Cause me to have no fellowship with the unfruitful works of darkness.

- Help me to walk in the spirit so I will not fulfil the lusts of the flesh.

- Let integrity and uprightness preserve me in the name of Jesus.

- Lord, I cast off the weights and sin that are in my life, in the name of Jesus.

- Father, help me to set my affections on the things which are above.

- Cleanse my heart and spirit of every kind and form of perversion.

- Dry up the thirst and craving that I have for anything sinful, in the name of Jesus.

- Father, I cast down imaginations and every high thing that I have set up in my mind, in the name of Jesus.

- Lord, I tear down every idol that is present in my life in the name of Jesus.

- Give me clean hands and a pure heart so I can receive promotions from you.

- Almighty God, I declare that I will not live below my privileges in the kingdom.

- Father, remove every kind and form of spiritual blindness from my life.

- Cause me not to grope and stumble in darkness, in the name of Jesus.

- Father, open my eyes to behold wonderful things in your word.

- Let the spirit of wisdom and revelation rest upon me in the name of Jesus.

- Flood the eyes of my understanding with knowledge, so I may understand the hope that I have in Christ.

- Father, I bind every spirit of confusion in the name of Jesus.

- Let clarity and divine direction come to my life in the name of Jesus.

- Remove the scales of pride and arrogance from my eyes, so I can accept your leading.

- Father, give me vision lest I perish.

- Father, I cast out everything that I have permitted into my life, which has polluted my spiritual vision.

- Help me to receive and maintain clear spiritual vision, in the name of Jesus.

- Lord, cause me to know you in the fellowship of your sufferings and to be made conformable unto your death.

- Father, I declare that I die daily in the name of Jesus.

- I am indeed crucified with Christ and I will not live to serve sin.

- May Christ be fully formed in me, so that I can say the god of this world, has nothing in me that belongs to him.

- Lord, I thank you for purging me for holy living in Jesus' name. Amen.

1.3 Lukewarmness

Scriptural Prayer Aids: Revelation 3:15-17, Romans 8:1,
*   Romans 12:2, I John 2:14-16*

Petition:

- Father, I thank you that you are the resurrection and the life.

- If any man believes in you though he is dead you will make him alive.

- Father, I prophesy over every dead area in my life and command them to receive life, in the name of Jesus.

- Lord I cast off dead weights from my life in the name of Jesus.

- I cancel every curse of death and hell from my life, in the name of Jesus.

- I declare, that I shall not die but live to see the glory of the Lord, in the land of the living.

- God, please restore unto me, the years that the palmer worm and canker worm have eaten up out of my life.

- Take me out of mere existence and propel me into purposeful living, in the name of Jesus.

- I bind every spirit of depression and suicide that wars against my mind in the name of Jesus.

- Lord revive me so I can call on your name.

- Renew my strength because I wait only for you.

- Anoint me with fresh oil and exalt my horn.

- Bring me into your divine will and cause me to prosper.

- Lord, I understand that seeking your face means seeking the greatest part of your person.

- So, today, I search out the strength of your character.

- It is written, that if I seek you with all my heart and soul I will find you.

- Therefore Father, I purpose in my spirit that I will seek you until I find you.

- Father, teach me how to seek out the deep things which are found in your presence.

- Holy God, release to me the hidden treasures of wisdom, which are found in Christ Jesus.

- Father, I thank you that you no longer dwell only in temples made by man but you dwell within me.

- Because God is holy then I profess today that I am holy.

- I declare that no other spirit will rule in this temple but the spirit of the living God.

- I sever every tie, with any familiar spirit, that has been passed down to me through my bloodline, in the name of Jesus.

- Father, help me to set my affections on the things which are above in the name of Jesus.

- Cleanse my heart and spirit of every kind and form of perversion.

- Cause me not to grope and stumble in darkness, in the name of Jesus.

- Father, open my eyes to behold wonderful things in your word.

- Let the spirit of wisdom and revelation rest upon me in the name of Jesus.

- Father, visit my foundation and purge me of every pollution in my spirit in the name of Jesus.

- Holy God, replace every virtue and spiritual strength that I have lost in the name of Jesus.

- I break every soul tie I have allowed in my life knowingly or unknowingly, in the name of Jesus

- Lord make me a vessel of honour this day in the name of Jesus.

- I plead the blood of Jesus over every doorway to my soul, in the name of Jesus.

- I close the door way of my ears, my eyes and mind to every lie of the enemy, in the name of Jesus.

- I break every covenant that I have made through negative thoughts and through surrounding myself with negative people.

- Fill me with the Holy Ghost and fire and cause my life to burn continually for you.

- Restore the zeal and passion I once had for the things of the kingdom.

- Please deliver me from the mechanics of dead religion, in the name of Jesus.

- Lord, take me out of my spiritual comfort zone and put me in hot pursuit of you.

- Father please energize my body, soul and spirit.

- Lord please revive my spirit and restore the joy of my salvation.

- Father help me to return to my first love with all of my heart.

- Lord, I thank you for your grace and the renewal that comes from your presence. In the name of the Lord Jesus. Amen.

1.4 Personal Strongholds

Scriptural Prayer Aids: Jeremiah 48:41, Mark 3:27, 2 Corinthians 10:3-5

Petition:

- Father, in the name of Jesus I thank you that when Jesus died on the cross He took captivity captive.

- I cast down every stronghold which I have built up in my mind that is contrary to your will, in the name of Jesus.

- Let every stronghold in my bloodline, which is militating against me, in the form of sickness and disease, utterly fall to irreparable pieces.

- I command every stronghold of tragedy, manifesting itself in my life, to be permanently destroyed, in the name of Jesus.

- Almighty God, defend my body, soul and spirit, in the name of Jesus.

- Be my strong habitation and refuge in the time of trouble.

- Let the stronghold of lack and poverty break from my life, in the name of Jesus.

- Let the stronghold of seasonal sickness and mental paralysis, break from over my life, in the name of Jesus.

- Lord, cause the stronghold of repetitive cycles of negative thoughts, tendencies and behaviour, to break from over my life, in the name of Jesus.

- Let every stronghold in my life be smashed against the rock of my salvation, in the name of Jesus.

- Father, I close every door which has given satan access to my life, in the name of Jesus.

- I rid myself of every kind of seduction that I have bought into, whether consciously or subconsciously.

- Father, make known to me anything in my home or environment that keeps strongholds alive in my life.

- Father, I repent if I have rejected your truth in one way or the other.

- I break myself loose from every kind and form of delusion, in the name of Jesus.

- Let pride and arrogance depart from me in the name of Jesus.

- God I refuse to walk in bitter envy, jealously, malice and selfish ambition.

- Great God, I cast down every idol which I have planted in my heart.

- I declare that you are the only Lord of my life and that I will bow down to no other god.

- Let your kingdom come in and through me, in the name of Jesus.

- I come against every negative word and action, which was planted in my consciousness as a child.

- Let every situation, which I have encountered in life, that has caused me to erect a stronghold, be covered by the blood of Jesus.

- Lord, let the spirit of fear not overtake and dominate my life, in the name of Jesus.

- Lord, let not regret and the thoughts and feelings which linger as a result of failure, take up residence in my life.

- Father, help me never to accept or to become comfortable, with the strongholds harboured in my life.

- God, cause me to turn towards you with my whole heart.

- Today, I surrender my body soul and spirit to you.

- Do what only you can Father, as I give you thanks, in Jesus' name. Amen.

1.5 Habitual Sin

Scriptural Prayer Aids: Romans 6:12-14, 1 John 1:9-10,
*   1 John 5:4-5*

Petition:

- Merciful father, I fall upon your grace right now, in the name of Jesus.

- I confess that I am weak but you are eternally strong.

- I surrender every fibre of my being to you, in the name of Jesus.

- Help O Lord! The waters of sin and death have come into my soul!

- I am sinking swiftly and deeply and cannot help myself.

- Lord God of my salvation, hear me speedily, in the name of Jesus.

- When I would do good my father, evil is present with me. I know that I break your heart every time I (mention the sin).

- You are bigger than any of my shortcomings and so I confess and repent of my shortcoming/s, in the name of Jesus.

- I place my transgression/s under the blood of Jesus and announce that there is no condemnation, to them who are truly in Christ Jesus.

- Father, I submit myself entirely to you, so that I will have the strength to resist the devil and his devices, in the name of Jesus.

- I confess that sin will no longer have dominion over me, in the name of Jesus.

- Father, remove the enticement that draws me into (mention the sin) the name of Jesus.

- Lord, help me to see sin the way you see it, in the name of Jesus.

- Father, help me to draw near to you so that you can draw near to me.

- Cleanse me from double-mindedness and help me to make a conscious decision to depart from iniquity.

- Father, deliver me from fear of the consequences, associated with giving up (mention the sin).

- Father, cleanse my environment of anything that keeps (mention the sin) alive, in the name of Jesus.

- Father, help me to examine my relationships and associations, to see if they are contributing factors to my constant downfall.

- Father, I thank you that you are my advocate and so I boldly stand against, every accusation of the enemy, in the name of Jesus.

- Lord, help me to keep myself from everything that would send me back into sin.

- Father, expose every snare and seduction of the enemy, in the name of Jesus.

- Help me to forget those things which are behind and to press towards the mark of the high calling, in Christ Jesus.

- I declare that I will not keep reliving the incident/s in my mind, in the name of Jesus.

- I have been forgiven and so I will not dwell in a state of unworthiness, in the name of Jesus.

- Lord, I sever every tie I have with (mention the sin), in the name of Jesus.

- The blood of Jesus cleanses thoroughly from sin and brings me back into relationship with God.

- I now walk in the liberty which is in Christ Jesus.

- I declare that I possess great peace, therefore nothing shall offend me.

- I pronounce that I have overcome habitual sin, by the blood of the Lamb.

- I believe, so I have spoken, let my words be framed in the heavens, in the name of Jesus.

- Father, thank you for your outstretched love and tender mercies. Amen.

1.6 Sexual Purity

Scriptural Prayer Aids: 1 Corinthians 6:18-19, Ephesians 5:3

Petition:

- Father, I thank you that you no longer dwell only in temples made by man but you dwell within me.

- I declare that no other spirit will rule in this temple but the spirit of the almighty God.

- I sever every tie with any familiar spirit, of a sexual orientation, that has been passed down to me through my bloodline, in the name of Jesus.

- Father, visit my foundation and purge me of every pollution which has resulted from rape, incest, molestation, inappropriate exposure to sex, heavily laced sexual encounters in the dream and the influence of sexual perversion in my environment, in the name of Jesus.

- Holy God, replace every virtue and spiritual strength that I have lost through indulging in sexual sin, in the name of Jesus.

- Lord make me a vessel of honour this day in the name of Jesus.

- I plead the blood of Jesus over every doorway to my soul, in the name of Jesus.

- Father, I thank you for my body and all of its functions which you designed.

- Lord, you commanded me to rule and have dominion over the earth and so I apply this commandment to my sexual desires.

- Help me to understand that there is nothing perverse about sexuality, as you created it by your good counsel.

- Help me to realize that like any other gift, sexuality comes with great responsibility.

- You ordained that it should be enjoyed within the confines of the blood covenant of marriage between a man and a woman.

- Therefore, I declare that my sexuality will not be tampered with, outside of your design.

- I declare that I will not yield my body as a tool of unrighteousness.

- Father, I renounce any engagement I have had with fornication whether in my mind, body or spirit, in the name of Jesus.

- I renounce any engagement I have had with adultery whether in my mind, body or spirit, in the name of Jesus.

- I ask Father, that you help me not to allow sexual thoughts to ensnare me.

- Help me not to open myself up to engaging in sexual encounters through my imagination.

- Father, I renounce any agreement I have made consciously or unconsciously with pornography, in the name of Jesus.

- I declare that my eye gate will not be a place to harbour perversion in the name of Jesus.

- I refuse to engage in any sex act without a God given partner, in the name of Jesus.

- The natural occurrences of sexual urges will not bring me to a place of mental, emotional or spiritual bondage.

- I take control of my myself and my environment.

- I refuse to allow anything into my life that will contaminate me, in the name of Jesus.

- I take a stand against gay, lesbian, bisexual,

transgender, trisexuality, bestiality thoughts and tendencies, in the name of Jesus.

- I agree with God, who ordained a sexual covenant to be shared between a biological man and a biological woman and any diversion from this truth, must be actively resisted.

- I declare that I will not run with the excesses of this world and its systems.

- Father, I thank you for releasing me from bondage and for making my body a living sacrifice for your glory. Amen.

1.7 Spiritual Thirst

Scriptural Prayer Aids: Psalm 42:1, Psalm 63, Isaiah 44:3, 64:1,
Acts 3:19

Petition:

- Fountain of living water, I come to you today in the name of Jesus.

- Almighty God, you promised to pour water on those who are thirsty and to send floods upon dry places.

- Father accomplish this word in my life and generation.

- Father, I am thirsty for your manifested presence. I am in desperate search of the spiritual wells that my forefathers dug.

- God, please give me the strength and drive to re-dig the wells of revival in this season.

- I pant after my rightful place in you. I long to find my purpose so I can walk in destiny.

- O God position me in your kingdom, and equip me to fulfil your will in every area of my life.

- Father, come unto me as the former and latter rains today, in the name of Jesus.

- Lord, visit the dry and parched places in my life and quench them with your Spirit.

- Father, satisfy the yearnings of my soul and grant unto me a season of refreshing.

- I set myself to seek you until the heavens become heavy with rain.

- I will cry out to you O God, until you visit me.

- Father, I will give you no rest, until the Spirit is poured out on me from on high.

- I will not eat in comfort or sleep at ease until I experience your glory.

- Father, now let the heavens be opened and send me a flood of your anointing because I will be satisfied with nothing less.

- As the waters rise in my favour, let them become as waters to swim in.

- Pour out on me in such measure, that the waters flow into the streets and give life to all those who come in contact with it.

- Let the glory that you pour out carry me into new territory.

- God, please lead me into your overflow and cause me to see you face to face.

- Father, I ask that you awaken me to the reality of where I am in time.

- Lord, position my generation to achieve what no other generation has achieved.

- O God, deliver me from careless living and casual Christianity, in the name of the Lord Jesus.

- Make plain paths for my feet and cause me to walk in your will.

- Cause me to shake myself and put on my strength, so that I will be able to stand.

- Father, cause me to be alert and watchful so that the enemy does not distract me.

- Teach me how to seek you until I find you.

- Deliver me from dead religion and the traditions of men.

- Take me out of spiritual stagnation and bring me into the reality of who you are.

- Take me out of self worship and cause me to return to godly worship.

- Cause me to rise out of spiritual sleep and slumber and take my rightful place in your kingdom.

- Father, I ask that you resurrect every dead vision, dream and gift that lies dormant in my life.

- Let this be the moment that I step into destiny in Jesus' name.

- God, I thank you for giving me rain in due season and I look forward to the harvest that will follow in Jesus' name. Amen.

1.8 Fruit of the Spirit

Scriptural Prayer Aids: John 15:8, Romans 8:14, Gal. 5:22-25

Petition:

- Father, I thank you that I can do nothing without you.

- Jesus, you are the True Vine and Almighty God is the husband man.

- I declare that I am abiding in the True Vine and nothing can uproot me.

- I declare that I will be a fruitful vine in the name of Jesus.

- Father, it is written that you will prune me in order for me to bring forth even more fruit.

- Lord, help me not to resist your pruning process in the name of Jesus.

- Almighty God, cause the love of God to be shed abroad in my heart.

- Let the love of God clothe me and manifest itself in every area of my life.

- Let the fruit of the Spirit manifest from my life in abundance, in the name of Jesus.

- Cause me to bear much fruit in the name of Jesus.

- Father, I ask that you help me to walk in the Spirit so that I do not fulfil the lust of the flesh.

- Holy Father, anoint me with fresh oil in the name of Jesus.

- Cause me to come into complete alignment with your plans and purposes for my life.

- Help me to know when my environment is being polluted by evil, in the name of Jesus.

- Teach me how to discern the wicked intentions of the enemy.

- Help me not to become entangled and distracted by the affairs of this life, in the name of Jesus.

- Help me to discern your will in every situation I may find myself in.

- Let my spiritual senses come alive and begin functioning in their full capacity, in the name of Jesus.

- Father visit me through, open visions and dreams, in the name of Jesus.

- Teach me how to ascend into the heavenly realms in the name of Jesus.

- Father, let the realm of the supernatural become more real to me, than the natural realm, in the name of Jesus.

- Release to me the things that eyes have not seen and ears have not heard and that which has yet to enter into the consciousness of man.

- Help me to discern your voice at all times, in the name of Jesus.

- Father show me how to live consistently in the Spirit.

- Make me a carrier of your glory in the name of Jesus.

- Let the weight of your glorious presence rest upon me each and every day in the name of Jesus.

- Let your kingdom manifest mightily through me, in the name of Jesus.

- Let everything in my life, that prevents me from walking in greatness begin to give way now, in the name of Jesus.

- Thank you for accomplishing your good pleasure in my life. Amen.

1.9 Stirring up Spiritual Gifts

Scriptural Prayer Aids: 1 Corinthians 12, Romans 12:4–8, Ephesians 4:11–16, 2 Timothy 1:6–7

Petition:

- Father in the name of Jesus I lift my soul before you.
- You knew everything about me before I was formed in my mother's womb you knew.
- Lord, you ordain my gifts and calling from the foundations of the world.
- So, I stand in your omniscience and ask that reveal to me the hidden gifts, talents, and abilities I have yet to discover.
- Let the spirit of wisdom and revelation be poured on me without measure and cause me to tap into your blueprint for my life.
- I prophesy to every dead and dormant gift, and I command them to come to life in Jesus' name.
- Father let your fire fall on my spiritual womb and set me ablaze for your glory.
- Baptize me again with the Holy Ghost and fire consume me with your zeal.
- Awaken me out of complacency and let my gifts emerge with newfound fervour.
- Energize me in your presence and fill me with a fresh hunger and thirst for your glory.
- Ignite my life and calling with your fire and break me free from all forms of lukewarmness.
- Lord break the spirit of fear and intimidation off of me and help me to express my gifts freely.
- Help me to maximize my calling and to search out the extremities of my gifts.
- Cause my gifts to make room for me and to bring me before great man.
- Father allow my gifts to prosper at every turn and make it impossible for me to fail.
- Let my path become slippery with the anointing and anoint me with fresh oil from every day.

- Teach me how to guard and protect my gifts. Help to prevent all forms of distortion and manipulation of my gifts and calling.
- Let me never underserve my talents and abilities and settle for less than you intend for me.
- Teach me how to define and refine my gifts and learn how to perfect what you have called me to be.
- Show me how to distinguish between my major and minor and gifts.
- Grant me good counsel so I will know what to major in and what to minor in.
- Once I activate my gifts let it be that there is never a decline in their demonstration and administration.
- Father, increase my capacity to handle greater dimensions of the expression and demonstration of my gifts.
- Lord, help me to plunge into the deep and to unearth all the treasure on the inside of me.
- Expose me in the light of your coming and cause me to see myself the way you do.
- Give me the unction to function effectively in my area of calling.
- Help me to recognize that my gifts are intended to serve others and to fulfill the mandate of the kingdom.
- Cause me never to be complacent with my gifts and help me to challenge myself to expand them and cause them to grow.
- Jesus gave himself to the world so help me to give myself unreservedly to my calling.
- Grant me the discipline I need to develop my gifts, talents, and abilities.
- Lord me help to run my race well by utilizing all that you have deposited in me.
- Lord let heavens be opened over my head and cause your glory to expand my gifts.
- Let signs and wonders become common place in my life.
- Increase my faith and grant me the boldness of the righteous to walk out my assignment.
- Cause a tangible weight of your presence and power to always reside over my gifts, my life, and my calling in Jesus' name.

1.10 Spiritual Vision

Scriptural Prayer Aids: Jeremiah 29 :11, Proverbs 29:18, Numbers 12:6, Habakkuk 2: 2-3
Petition:

- Father in the name of Jesus I ask that you remove all spiritual scales from my eyes.
- Give me vision so that my dreams, aspirations, sense of direction and purpose do not perish.
- Open my eyes to behold wondrous things out of your law.
- Let your word become a lamp to my feet and a light to my path.
- Make plain paths for my feet and direct my life with your mighty hand.
- Father, I ask that you reveal the blueprint you have for my life.
- Fill me with the spirit of wisdom and revelation and give me insight in all areas of my life.
- Enlighten the dark areas of my life and cause me to be delivered from personal ignorance.
- Reveal the purpose for my life and teach me how to harness your perfect will for my life.
- Show me how to lay a solid foundation for my vision and how to bring it to life.
- Lord let my destiny helpers emerge to help me to get the vision off the ground.
- Sharpen my spiritual senses and help to discern your voice at every stage of the vision.
- Father expose every vision killer in my life in Jesus' name.
- I come against fear and intimidation as I step out to fulfill the vision in my heart.
- Father let all barriers be broken down and lift every spiritual embargo erected against my vision.
- Lord release the strategy that will lead to vision fulfillment.

- Show me how to get this vision off paper and into manifestation.
- Cause my faith not to waver when challenges emerge with my vision.
- Help me to tap into the prophetic and be able to see this vision the way you see it.
- Position me to build generationally through my vision and to set the stage for its duplication.
- Let this vision unlock things that have been withheld from by bloodline for generations.
- Cause it to break evil family patterns and to establish a generational blessing in Jesus' name.
- Let this vision continue speaking long after I am gone and let it become a signal to the enemy that my mark will remain.
- Father bring me into the dimension of inventions and let this vision become world changing.
- Almighty God do through me what has never been done in the earth before.
- Cause me to tap into the things that eyes have not seen and ear have not heard, and that which is yet to enter the consciousness of man.
- Father, I declare that I will not abort this vision but that I will carry it to full-term in Jesus' name.
- Order every step and stage and cause my feet never to slip off the path of the vision.
- Help me not to get discouraged when opposers emerge to frustrate my vision but to remain resolute in its realization.
- Lord strengthen my spiritual loins to give birth to this vision and to nurture it continually in Jesus' name.

1.11 Spiritual Mantles
Scriptural Prayer Aids: *I Kings 19: 19-21, 2 Kings 2:8*
Petition:

- Father in the name of Jesus I ask that you reveal and release the mantles assigned to my life.

- Reveal the full measure of my jurisdiction and the capacity of my mantle.

- Teach me how to grow in the full stature of my mantle.

- Lord help me to walk in alignment with my God-given assignments.

- Let the mantle open doors for me that no man can shut.

- Cause it to break down barriers, remove restrictions and destroy satanic embargos positioned against my calling.

- Father rush divine favour, influence, affluence, and access to me through my mantle.

- As I strike my mantle, cause every Red Sea of opposition to part in the name of Jesus.

- Lord let my mantle become a shield against the arrows of the enemy in the name of Jesus.

- Reveal to me the measure of authority and power deposited in my mantle.

- Let transformation come to the lives of all those who come in contact with the mantle.

- Father reveal the rank and seat of power I am privileged to walk in with my mantle.

- Let the heavens open and cause divine intelligence to enlighten every dark area of my life.

- Father let the mantle begin to make pathways for my family, bloodline, and generations.

- Let it stir my spiritual sons and daughters and cause them to emerge from the four corners of the earth.

- Cause them to be shaken into position and to do great exploits in the earth.

- Lord grant them a double portion of your spirit and power in Jesus' name, amen.

1.12 Spiritual Jurisdictions

Scriptural Prayer Aids: Nehemiah 3:7, Luke 20:20, Luke 23:7
Petition:

- Father in the name of Jesus cause me to come into the territory you have designated for my spiritual DNA to lodge in Jesus' name.

- As I discover and walk into it, my footprint, handprint, and voiceprint, activate the assignments and angels needed to guard and preserve the territory.

- Lord cause a wall of fire to be consistently around my borders.

- Father may the enemy never take root in the place where you have planted me in Jesus' name.

- Cause the desire of the wicked concerning my place of power to be perpetually frustrated in Jesus' name.

- I take jurisdictional authority over my family, and I declare that as for me and my house we will serve the Lord.

- I decree that the law of the Lord will not depart from my bloodline for all generations unborn to time.

- I command the angels assigned to the fulfillment of my destiny to begin to emerge.

- Father let them mark the territory you have given me and become a wall of fire around it.

- Almighty God, as a build an altar unto you in this place let it become a memorial between us for my generations.

- By your power help me to operate wisely in my jurisdiction.

- May the territory that I have gained never be taken away in the mighty name of Jesus.

- Almighty God, let your peace be continually in my borders and joy within my walls.

- Let no form of violence, upheaval, sabotage, or confusion be once named within my jurisdiction.

- Lord, I thank you for the territory and grace to rule and reign from my seat of power, in Jesus' name.

PART II

PROSPERITY

Prosperity of the Soul

It is the will and delight of our Father that we prosper in every area of our lives. Poverty is a curse, whether it be poverty of mind, body, or spirit. Every believer has been given access to the vast provision, which God has for those who love Him. We should, therefore, embrace God's plan for our lives through prayer. When our ways please Him there is nothing, He will withhold from us!

2.1 Mind & Emotions

Scriptural Prayer Aids: Proverbs 4:23, Isaiah 26:3,

Roms. 8:6, 3 John vs. 2

Petition:

- Lord, I send into captivity, every thought pattern and mental bondage that has kept me in chains, in the name of Jesus.

- Father, I cast down imaginations and every high thing that seeks to exalt itself, against the knowledge of who you are in my life.

- I will only listen to the voice of God and the voice of a stranger I will not follow.

- Father, cause every spirit of torment that the enemy has sent against my life, to be permanently frustrated.

- I declare that I possess the mind of Christ, in the name of Jesus.

- Father, I rid myself of every spirit of fear and guilt, in the name of Jesus Christ.

- I come against depression and despair in the name of Jesus.

- I refuse to entertain negative thoughts which help to build up strife between me and God.

- I refuse to allow my mind to be corrupted by the systems of this world, in the name of Jesus.

- I confess that I will be continually transformed, by the renewing of my mind.

- Today, I put on the helmet of salvation, as a shield against the poisonous mental arrows, which the enemy sends my way.

- Purge me Father, from any rejection or hostility that I may have encountered from the womb.

- Father cause the law of my mind to be subjected to the law of your Spirit.

- Father, let faith become my fortress and not my intelligence and reasoning ability.

- I stand against every kind and form of beguilement, sent against my life by the enemy, in the name of Jesus.

- I refused to be ensnared and enslaved by the pressures of this world.

- I refuse to be distracted and thrown off course from my destiny, by unprofitable thinking in the name of Jesus

- I come against every kind of mind blankness and aimless thinking, in the name of Jesus.

- I come against worry, anxiety, confusion and stressful thinking in the name of Jesus.

- Father, I place my entire emotional trauma before you and I ask that you remove it, in the name of Jesus.

- Lord, heal me of every emotional wound I have ever suffered, in the name of Jesus.

- Rid me of unforgiveness, bitterness and hatred.

- Father, please, let nothing in my past prevent me from loving others and opening myself up to receive love, in the name of Jesus.

- Father, let the damage that I have done to my own emotions and mind, be repaired by the blood of the Lamb. Amen.

2.2 Wisdom

Scriptural Prayer Aids: Job 28:28, Psalm 49:3, Proverbs 2:6-8, Isaiah 33:6

Petition:

- Father, I thank you that all the treasures of wisdom are hid in Christ Jesus.

- Because of the shed blood of Jesus Christ I have access to all these treasures.

- Father, teach me how to dig for the secret riches that are found in wisdom.

- Almighty God, fill me with the spirit of wisdom and revelation, in the name of Jesus.

- Cause the eyes of my understanding to be opened, so that I may know the glorious riches of your inheritance.

- Entrust me with wisdom beyond my years and experience, in Jesus' name.

- Father, make me wiser than my teachers, in the name of Jesus.

- Anoint me with superior and excellent wisdom above my companions.

- Give me prudence and insight into the mysteries of your will.

- Reveal your manifold wisdom to me, so your eternal purpose for my life can be fulfilled.

- Teach me how to walk in wisdom and cause my words to be filled with knowledge and understanding.

- Anoint my ears so I can hear the voice of wisdom everywhere I go.

- Bring me into your counsel so that I can make intelligent decisions for my life.

- Cause wisdom to enter into my heart, and let knowledge become pleasant to my soul.

- Father, give me the strength that comes with finding wisdom.

- Let it become a shield and a refuge for me in the day of trouble.

- Father grant me the wealth and honour that come with possessing wisdom.

- Let wisdom never depart from my life in the name of Jesus.

- Lord, cause me to leave a legacy of wisdom, knowledge and understanding for my children's children.

- I ask that you give me the wisdom to recognize and to embrace all that you have for me.

- May all the opportunities and promotions that come with finding wisdom, be my portion, in the name of Jesus.

- Lord let foolishness and unprofitable speaking depart from me, in the name of Jesus.

- Lord cause my words to give direction and insight to those around me.

- Lord make a way for the wisdom that you have invested in me to cause men to enquire of you.

- Father, let my display of wisdom glorify your name in the earth.

- Almighty God, I ask that the portion of wisdom that I have received will be a defence for my life.

- Length of days and peace shall be my portion, in the land of the living, in the name of Jesus.

- Father, please grant me favour with men of all walks of life in the name of Jesus.

- Father, help me to trust in you with all my heart and not lean to my own understanding.

- Help me to delight in instruction and to have pleasure in correction, in the name of Jesus.

- Help me to flee from the foolishness of pride and arrogance, in the name of Jesus.

- Let not wealth, accomplishment and advancement become idols in my life.
- Father, I thank you for giving me wisdom for everyday living . Amen.

2.4 Self-Esteem

Scriptural Prayer Aids: Psalm 139:14, Psalm 149:4, Isaiah 49:15-16, I Peter 3:3-4

Petition:

- Father, I thank you that I am fearfully and wonderfully made.

- Today, I agree with and wholeheartedly believe your thoughts towards me.

- God I am grateful that I am the apple of your eye and that my name is written in the palm of your hand.

- Thank you that you are always with me and that you will never forsake me.

- Because of your love I can receive forgiveness and help to walk through anything.

- Father I am assured that because I am your child I am special.

- You promised to beautify your children with salvation and I thank you for doing it for me.

- Father I repent of depending on my own strength and allowing my thoughts to centre entirely on me.

- Today I will keep my mind on you and I rest in the knowledge that my beauty, strength and ability does not come from me, but from you.

- I exchange my identity to receive my identity in Christ.

- Lord please restore the joy of your salvation to my life.

- Help me to cast all my cares on you on a daily basis.

- Cause me to find fullness of joy in your presence.

- Strengthen my faith to trust you in every situation.

- Father give me a new beginning and remove all my doubts and fears.

- Help me to accept myself for who I am and not to try to become someone else.

- Help me to resist every feeling of inferiority that the devil will try to send against me.

- God uncover every lie and deception of satan that I have accepted.

- God of war, break every chain and remove every obstacle that seeks to trap me.

- Teach my hands how to war and my fingers how to fight, for my peace of mind and contentment.

- Father, I declare today that I am the head and not the tail.

- Help me to find my confidence in you, in the name of Jesus Christ.

- Father, I wait for and gladly receive affirmation from you, in the name of Jesus.

- Lord even if my mother and father forsake me you promised to take me up.

- Help me not to be ashamed of my past or my present situation.

- Father, I renounce every negative word that has been spoken to me, which is presently affecting my self-esteem.

- Give me freedom from the captivity of hurtful and cruel words, in the name of Jesus.

- Cause my mind to be renewed daily in your presence, in Jesus' name.

- Help me to discover true beauty which can only come from my spirit.

- Help me to make every effort to ensure that my spirit man is beautified, through attending to spiritual things, in the name of Jesus.

- Father let the light of your glory shine forth from my face, in the name of Jesus.

- Father, reveal the reality of my position in you, in the name of Jesus.

- Lord, transform me into your image and cause the beauty of Jesus to be seen in me.

- I declare that I will not descend from the high estate that I have in Christ.

- Today, I make the decision never to allow myself to feel less than what you ordained me to be.

- Mighty God, I thank you for renewed hope, assurance and victory in Jesus' name. Amen.

2.5 Trauma & Abuse

Scriptural Prayer Aids: I Peter 5:7, Isaiah 41: 10, Psalm 107:13-16, Psalm 34:4.

- Father in the name of Jesus I look to you today as my Balm in Gilead.

- Heal me O God and I will be healed, save me and I will be saved.

- Lord, deliver me from all forms of abuse I have suffered in my lifetime.

- Peel back the scars and the places that wounds are still festering in my soul and heal me on a foundational level.

- Erase all forms of psychological damage and the memories that hold me captive.

- I reclaim everybody part that was sold into sexual bondage in the name of Jesus.

- I expel the residue of any initiation into acts of perversion through past experiences.

- Every covenant I have entered consciously or subconsciously with spirits of trauma and abuse be broken now in the name of Jesus.

- Let me not harbour bitterness or hatred towards my abusers.

- Free my mind, body, and spirit from past pain in Jesus' name.

- Let no negative word that was spoken over me while I was broken stand.

- Lord, purge my belief system concerning who I am and the value you have placed on me.

- Almighty God, let every mark of ridicule, downgrading, inferiority, insecurity, and shame be rubbed off my life permanently by the blood of Jesus.

- Lord of Hosts let the gatekeepers of the prisons of condemnation, hopelessness, helplessness, crippling cycles, negative emotions, and self-sabotage fall and die.

- As I lift my soul to you in prayer, let the shackles begin to fall.

- Lord let there be turbulence in the heavens and upon the earth as my chains begin to break.

- Let those who have damaged me lose their power over me in the name of Jesus.

- Lord, I recall every virtue stolen out of my life by persons who preyed on me.

- Father help me to shake off every spiritual parasite that has attached itself to me because of evil environments I have been exposed to.

- Let all forms of spiritual disfigurement and damage be permanently erased from my in Jesus' name.

- Let my face begin to shine with your glory in the name of Jesus.

- Let no residue of my past hinder or pollute my future in the mighty name of Jesus.

- I arrest every spirit of trauma and abuse that has attacked me and declare that the doors are shut forever by the blood of the Lamb.

- Let no negative cycle of abuse or trauma repeat itself in my life or bloodline for all generations unborn to time.

- Now Father, I stand in the victory and authority of the shed blood of the Lamb and declare that I am free.

- My mind, spirit and body have been made free by the power of the living God.

- Right now, I permanently walk in the liberty that is in Christ Jesus and refuse to ever be bound again in Jesus' name, amen.

2.6 The Spirit of Fear

Scriptural Prayer Aids: Psalm 27:1, Psalm 56:3, 2 Timothy 1:7, Isaiah 43:1

- Almighty God, I thank you that you are omnipotent and that there is nothing you cannot deliver me from.

- Lord, I come against fear, and everything associated with it in the name of Jesus.

- Father break the power of all forms of fear transferred to me from the womb in Jesus' name.

- I arrest all forms of panic and anxiety warring against my peace.

- Father, please repair all damage done to my organs, mind, and emotions because of fear.

- Let the fortress that fear has built in my life be destroyed now in the name of Jesus.

- Let the incident/s that introduced me to the spirit of fear loose its/their hold over me and be erased from my consciousness, in Jesus' name.

- Father, I address every phobia in my life with the blood of Jesus.

- I arrest the paralyzing effects of fear manifesting in any area of my life, in the name of Jesus.

- Let the boldness that belongs to the righteous overrule all forms of timidity warring against my soul.

- Let the strongman of fear be stripped of his armour, his weapons rendered powerless, and his habitation made perpetually desolate in Jesus' name.

- Cause the cycle of fear to break off my family and bloodline for all generations.

- By the power of your might, completely frustrate the assignment and agenda of the spirit of fear.

- Restore the territory and blessings that fear has stolen out of my life a hundred-fold.

- Let this chapter of my life be filled with your peace, joy and confidence.

- May the doors that fear caused me not to walk through swing wide open for me in this season.

- Help me to live a life of absolute faith in Jesus' name.

- Let opposition or challenge I will face in the future cause me not to resort to opening myself to the spirit of fear.

- Father cause my newfound boldness to bring me into new spiritual territory.

- Open doors for me that no man can shut and cause these doors never to close on my family or bloodline.

- As I enter the realm of boldness let nothing that you have reserved for me be held back in this season.

- For your glory's sake help me to walk in dominion and to subdue in all areas of my life in Jesus' name.

2.7 Disappointment & Regret

Scriptural Prayer Aids: *Psalm 18:3, 2 Corinth. 4:8-9, Philippians 3:13-14*

- Father in the name of Jesus I lift the reality of who you are above the current disappointments and regrets in my life.
- I ask that you deliver me from negative mental cycles and from thoughts that consistently hold me hostage.
- Help me to let go of the past and get the courage to move forward.
- Lord, I refuse to allow regret to fuel hatred and bitterness in my heart for others.
- Keep me from rehearsing the shame and hurtful memories of past failure.
- I come against the crippling efforts of doubt and fear and declare that I will rise again.
- Though my bones may be dry I dare to prophesy that I will live.
- I reject the lies of the enemy that desire to convince me that I am a failure.
- I walk back into every section of the incidents, and I nullify their effects on my mind, emotions, and spirit.
- By the power of your right hand break the power of the spirit of failure from over my life.
- I refuse to remain in a place of perpetual sorrow concerning this matter.
- Father, I declare that my steps are ordered by you and because of this all things will work together for my good.
- I thank you that every situation that comes into my life is in your jurisdiction.
- According to your tender mercies and grace launch my life forward by your hand of fire.
- I declare that old things have passed away and all things have become new in Jesus' name, amen.

2.8 Grief

Scriptural Prayer Aids: Psalm 34:18, Psalm 73:26, Matthew 5:4

- Lord, I call to you and ask that you rush deliverance to my soul.

- Lord you are the God who can heal me of all wounds give me a remedy for my pain in Jesus' name.

- Father search out the places in my soul where grief has overtaken and release me.

- As I pour out my soul before you bring swift breakthrough in the mighty name of Jesus.

- Arise O God as the Lord of all comfort and cause me to receive overcoming comfort in Jesus 'name.

- Father, wipe all tears from my eyes and cause me to see your purpose unfolding even amid my pain.

- Lord, I cast all my pain on you now, lift its weight off me in Jesus' name.

- Deliver me from replaying the events that lead to my grief.

- Give me the courage to move forward from the tragedy of losing my loved one/s.

- Lord do not allow grief to override my ministry, gifts and calling in Jesus' name.

- Father let no situation that resulted in grief cause me to question your integrity and character.

- Father grant me overcoming power to get passed this season in my life.

- Let no seed of bitterness and revenge germinate in my heart because of sorrow.

- Deliver me from the crippling effects of grief and sorrow in Jesus' name.

- Father let no spirit of despair overtake me and cause no one to take advantage of me in my sorrow.

- Lord hide me in the secret place of your pavilion until these calamities pass over me.

- I tap into supernatural joy and that will overrule lingering spirits of grief and heartache.

- I refuse to be crippled mentally, emotionally, or spiritually because of my grief.

- I will not become a shell or go into mere existence because of grief.

- By the power of the Holy Ghost and break the yoke of grief and commission my unconditional release from its hold over me.

- Lord, I refuse to allow the spirit of grief to have unrestrained access to my family members.

- Father, I call out to you on their behalf, and ask that you raise them out of the place of affliction in Jesus' name.

- I resist the pit of grief that is designed to cover me with distress and to cause my soul to sink.

- Help me not to neglect my relationship with you or to become spiritually careless because of grief.

- Teach me how to guard my soul and spirit as I go through the grieving process.

- Father, I refuse to lay my vision and spiritual assignment down at the feet of grief.

- Lord let no form of grief derail me or cause me to detour from my destiny.

- I will not abort my purpose and destiny because grief and sorrow in Jesus' name.

- Father strengthen my feeble knees and cause your strength to become perfected in my weakness.

- By your grace help me to rise out of this situation stronger, wiser, and more spiritually resilient.

- As I move forward Lord command your lovingkindness in the daytime and cause your song never to depart from me at night in Jesus' name.

2.9 Depression

Scriptural Prayer Aids: Psalm 9:9, Psalm 30:11, Isaiah 41 :10

- Lord to you I lift up my soul, hear my cry and urgently attend to my prayer.
- Father, I ask that you rush help to me because the floods of depression have entered my soul.
- Lord today I declare that depression and everything associated with it must be eradicated from my life in Jesus' name.
- By your mercies deliver my eyes from tears and my feet from falling.
- Let the yoke of depression be destroyed by the anointing in the mighty name of Jesus.
- Cause the burdens of helplessness and hopelessness to be removed from my shoulders and restore my strength.
- Let the barrenness associated with depression be broken off my life in Jesus' name.
- Restore my taste, for food, water, and life in the mighty name of Jesus.
- Let negative mood swings associated with depression be lifted off me.
- Lord let every illegal soul-tie I have created that makes me feel that I cannot live without an individual be permanently broken in Jesus' name.
- Father, I declare that as of now, no human being will be allowed to build any negative strongholds in my life in Jesus' name.
- Lord, restore my soul and cause me to recover myself, my dreams, and possibilities.
- Help me not to sabotage God-ordained relationships because of depression.
- Lord, I cast all the pain, regret and disappointment that persistently lingers in my subconscious on you.

- I cast down every element of depression that I have elevated or magnified above the knowledge of who you are.
- Let my vision not be distorted or corrupted by depression in Jesus' name.
- I cast the spirit of depression out of my life and command it roots to be destroyed by the fire of the living God.
- Any attempt of the enemy to pollute my gene pool with this spirit will be perpetually frustrated in Jesus 'name.
- Lord, I destroy the habitation and feeding ground of depression right now.
- Let all its resources dry up and its safety net be broken and destroyed.
- I declare that deep depression will never take root in my life again in Jesus' name.
- By the shed blood of the Lamb, I order a shift over my mindset and emotional life.
- Lord help me to examine myself and see the patterns and tendencies that easily cause me to fall prey to depression.
- Teach me how to build up a defense in these areas and to keep them heavily guarded through prayer.
- Lord give me the grace to let go of anyone or anything that keeps depressive thoughts and tendencies alive in my life in Jesus' name.
- I prophesy to the four winds of heaven and command them to blow away the residue of any depressive encounters I have had at any point in my life.
- Lord today please give me my daily provision of joy, fill my mouth with laughter and cause me to enter your rest.
- I replace every garment of heaviness with garments of praise in Jesus' name.

- Lord, I thank you for being my strength, song, and salvation, amen.

2.10 Spirit of Suicide

Scriptural Prayer Aids: 1 Samuel 31:3-5, St. John 10:10, Romans 8:1-2

- Lord let every covenant I have made with the spirit of suicide consciously or subconsciously be broken now in Jesus' name.
- Father let the spirit of death, hell and the grave be rebuked from my mind, soul, and body.
- In this very moment I pass from death into life.
- I come against every lie and deception of the wicked one.
- Lord, I rebuke every spirit of untimely death and tragedy hunting after my soul.
- I disassociate myself from every desire to die before the appointed time in Jesus' name.
- I command every tormenting spirit bombarding my mind so that I will end my life, be rebuked, and cast down by the fire of God.
- Lord of Hosts let your sword be drawn against the workers of iniquity and those attempting to manipulate my destiny.
- Let the spirit of suicide be bound with fetters of iron and be cast into the abyss.
- By the power of your might let invading spirits be cast down and rendered powerless.
- At your rebuke O Lord let the eaters of flesh and drinkers of blood be destroyed.
- Let every predatory spirit that is strengthened by the shedding of blood receive sudden destruction.
- Lord cause your net to catch the feet of every hunter of my life.
- Everything and everyone in league with the spirit of death and hell in my life, depart now in Jesus' name.
- Father, I repair the breach in my spiritual life that invited the spirit of suicide in.

- Let the breach be sealed up for all generations to come in Jesus' name.
- Almighty God deliver me from suicidal thoughts and tendencies.
- Help me to break the cycle of escapism and a lack of endurance that makes me resort to thinking that the only solution to my problems is to stop living.
- Let my hatred for life be turned into a deep and unquenchable desire to live.
- Father remind me of the power of my calling and the plans you have for me.
- Show me how to fight for my life in Jesus' name.
- Cause all forms of self-hatred to break from my consciousness.
- Whatever legal ground the devil has over me concerning this matter let it be overruled, overturned, and destroyed.
- By the power of your might, I will live and not die in Jesus' name.
- Lord help me to identify and rid my mind, home and surroundings of everything that will trigger thoughts and desires to end my life.
- Father, I declare that I shut the door forever against all these occurrences and I refuse to return to them.
- Lord strengthen me with might in my innerman and grant me overcoming power in Jesus' name.
- Release into the realm of life and life more abundantly in the mighty name of Jesus.
- Help me to maximize my moments, days, opportunities, and purpose in Jesus' name.
- Now, Father, I give you praise and glory for your power to make me whole in Jesus' name.

2.11 New Beginnings

Scriptural Prayer Aids: Isaiah 43:19, Romans 7:6, I Corinthians 2:9-10, 2 Corinthians 5:17

Petition:

- God, I thank you that you are the God of new beginnings.

- Lord I thank you that you are the one who opens and no man can shut.

- I ask that you open new doors for me in the name of Jesus.

- Cause me to know the new things you are about to reveal in the earth.

- Make known to me the mysteries of your kingdom, so that I may walk in dominion.

- Lord, give me the hidden riches of dark places, and cause me to tap into the wealth of the wicked.

- May my years that have been eaten up by the palmer worm, caterpillar and cankerworm, be restored a hundred fold today, in Jesus' name.

- With this restoration, may I ascend into heights in you that my forefathers never knew.

- O Lord, reveal yourself to me in a way you have never done before and send me a tangible measure of your glory.

- Give me fresh vision, insight and revelation for my life.

- Father cause me to lie down in green pastures and lead me beside still waters for your name's sake.

- May I be filled with the knowledge of your will concerning every area of my life.

- Strengthen me with might in my inner man for my battles.

- Grant me the wisdom of intelligent warfare that I may triumph over the enemy.

- Lord of Hosts, cause me to pursue and overtake the enemy in all of my endeavours.

- Lion of Judah, send the fear and the dread of God before me, so that nations will submit to me.

- Before I call answer and while I am yet speaking bring my dreams and desires to pass.

- May the newness that I find today, remain with me throughout my lifetime and continue to produce fruit, even to a thousand generations.

- Father, I desire to break into new ground in the spirit.

- Deliver me from old mindsets and mental stagnation, in the name of the Lord Jesus.

- I declare that I am in a new season and that today is a new day.

- Old things are passed away and through your grace you will make all things new.

- Father, make me a new wine skin so that you can pour new wine into my life.

- Father, make me an active participant in the new things you are doing in the earth.

- Help me never to settle for what I have already experienced in you.

- Cause me to consistently and actively pursue you in your freshness.

- Father please renew my strength and youth like that of the eagle's.

- Lord I ask that you open my heart and spirit up to new possibilities in the world I live in.

- Cause me to reproduce the newness you have given me everywhere I go.

- Able God, grant my supplication according to your divine will and purpose, amen.

2.12 Favour & Elevation

Scriptural Prayer Aids: Exodus 12:36, I Samuel 2:26, Psalm 5:12, Proverbs 13:15

   Petition:

- Father, I thank you that promotion does not come from the east or the west, but that it comes from you.

- In your hand is the power to demote and to promote, Holy Father.

- Lord, I declare that I am in a season of multiple promotions.

- Father, cause the works of my hands to prosper, in the name of Jesus.

- Lord, make me a lender and not a borrower, in the name of Jesus.

- Cause me to be in the right place at the right time.

- Father, do exceedingly abundantly and far above anything I could ever think or ask.

- Overwhelm me with your blessing, provision and favour, in the name of Jesus.

- Lord, grant me I beseech you, the accomplishment of years in days.

- Give me in days what it would take years to handle and possess, in the name of Jesus.

- Lord, I break myself free from every kind of limitation, doubt and unbelief, in the name of Jesus.

- Resurrect my potentials and increase my capacity for greatness, in the name of Jesus.

- Bring me into greatness today in the name of Jesus.

- Let multiple promotions and favour be my portion in the land of the living.

- Father cause me to always partake of the goodness of the land.

- What would have become a curse to me make it a blessing.

- What would have become a trap for me make it a stepping stone.

- Prepare for me a table of provision and blessing in the presence of my enemy, for your name's sake.

- Make my name great and credible in the earth in the name of Jesus.

- Let prosperity of mind, body and spirit be my portion all the days of my life.

- I will lay down in peace and my sleep shall be sweet.

- Father, because the blessing of the Lord makes rich and adds no sorrow to it, I shall not be tormented or perplexed by the acquisition of material wealth.

- I prophesy into my tomorrow and I declare that the days which are to come, will be the best days of my life, in the name of Jesus.

- I speak into the heavens today and I command the resources which are laid up there to be released to me.

- I command the money that I own to multiply a thousand fold, in the name of Jesus.

- I release the blessings of the Lord over my family members, in the name of Jesus.

- I speak to every dead dream and vision in my life and I command them to come alive, in the name of Jesus.

- Fill me with spiritual substance and cause me to walk in divine revelation.

- Holy One, please restore lost time, energy and goods, in the name of Jesus.

- Father, I ask that you open the windows of heaven and pour me out a blessing that I will not have room to receive.

- Empower me with wealth yielding ideas and practices, for your name's sake.

- I declare that I will not labour in vain, in the name of Jesus.

- I command all devourers to vanish from my labour, in the name of Jesus.

- Father, please bring me into your wealthy place, in the name of Jesus.

- Lord, thank you for your favour and divine elevation. Amen.

2.13 Abundant Living

Scriptural Prayer Aids: Psalm 37:11, Prov. 3: 9-10, 11:28, John 10:10

Petition:

- Father open my ears to hear the sound of your coming, in the name of Jesus.

- Let the flood of your presence invade every area of my life, in the name of Jesus.

- Let heaven manifest forcefully on the earth through my life, in the name of Jesus.

- Cause the overflow of your presence and power to manifest in my life, in the name of Jesus.

- Penetrate me with your glory in the name of Jesus.

- Captivate my mind and will in the name of Jesus.

- Let prosperity become effortless for me in the name of Jesus.

- In the light of your glorious presence, let every measure of darkness in my life give way.

- Let every hard and dry place in my life receive refreshing in the name of Jesus.

- Let the glory that was promised to the last day church manifest mightily in my life.

- Make it impossible for the enemy to consistently stand before me.

- Cause the fire of your presence to ignite my spirit in the name of Jesus.

- Elevate me through your name Wonderful in the name of Jesus.

- Holy Father, magnify yourself through me in this season in the name of Jesus.

- Bring me back to the place I originally had in you from creation, in the name of Jesus.

- Let edenic glory, power and dominion manifest mightily in my life, in the name of Jesus.
- Father, grant me the closeness that Adam and Eve had with you before the fall.
- Let the limitless power of intelligence that Adam walked in become my reality.
- Take me to a place in you where time does not matter, in the name of Jesus.
- Let my words carry the sound of heaven in them.
- Lord, cause me to be a multiplier of your goodness in the earth.
- Father, because I am seated in heavenly places in Christ Jesus, principalities and powers will not rule over me.
- Lord, I thank you that your angels are ever encamping round about me.
- Let my very presence rebuke and confound the enemy, in the name of Jesus.
- Father, let my life be ever engaged in your presence and power, in the name of Jesus.
- Father today, I step into a seven-fold, yoke destroying anointing, in the name of Jesus Christ.
- I call back every blessing that my family has lost over the last hundred years, in the name of Jesus.
- I declare today, that the generational blessings which were intended for my family, will begin to manifest right now.
- I call back every lost dream, opportunity and virtue that has gone from my life, in the name of Jesus.
- Let the royal splendour given to a king manifest in my life.
- Let the words of this prayer be established in the heavens, in the name of Jesus.

- Lord, thank you for visiting me with the strength of your glory, may my life never remain the same, Amen.

2.14 Divine Connections

Scriptural Prayer Aids: Esther 4, Acts 8:27-40, Luke 23:26

- Father in the name of Jesus I ask that you root out every imposter in my life and replace them with those aligned to my purpose.
- Lord, I revoke the right of the enemy to use the people entering my life as evil diversions.
- Let no form of imposter syndrome keep me from ascending to the heights you have called me to walk in.
- I come against every masquerading spirit lingering in my life and command them to be cast out in the name of Jesus.
- I speak into the womb of every day of the rest of this year and declare that they must give birth to my God-ordained connections.
- Lord help me to be in the right place at the right time in the name of Jesus.
- I ask that you cause me to tap into the magnetism of the anointing.
- Help me to attract those you have assigned to bring good things into my life.
- Lord by your power repel everyone that is coming with an evil or ulterior motive in Jesus' name.
- Father by the power of your might connect me in the right rooms, industries, and systems.
- Let the spirit of wisdom and revelation rest on me and reveal the people who are anointed to bring essential connections into my life.
- Father align me with divine purpose and cause my steps to be order according to your perfect will.

- Almighty God, I thank you for being my director and eternal guide in Jesus' name.

2.15 Destiny Helpers

*Scriptural Prayer Aids: 1 Samuel 18:1, I Kings 19: 19-21,
St. John 1:19-34*

- Almighty God, you are one who rules in the affairs of men and have ordered happenings, as well as times and seasons.

- Cause my entire life to come into agreement with your appointed times and seasons.

- Let my path become slippery with the anointing and cause me to ride on the high places of the earth.

- Father launch me into the realm of destiny in Jesus' name.

- Take hold of shield and buckler concerning my destiny and defend my cause in the earth.

- Plead my cause O God and fight against those who fight against my destiny in Jesus' name.

- Let everything in the in the cosmos align with your plans and purpose for my life.

- I come against every human, systematic and demonic detention tactic opposing my destiny.

- I rebuke all forms of demonic memory loss attacking my destiny helpers in Jesus' name.

- Let no evil communication be released against my purpose and destiny by anyone at any time.

- Father cause no strange wind to divert my destiny helpers from me in the name of Jesus.

- Lord, I declare that no evil counsel concerning my destiny will stand in the name of Jesus.

- Let those who rise against your plans and purpose for me be brought to perpetual disgrace.

- Cause the magnetic pull of your Spirit to begin to automatically attract my destiny helpers to me in Jesus' name.

- I prophesy to the four winds and command them to begin to blow my destiny helpers in my direction.

- I take dominion over the jurisdiction designated for the fulfillment of my destiny and I uproot every demonic seed planted there.

- Let every place, system, and structure, you cause my feet to tread down, become places of power and authority for me.

- I arrest every legal and illegal entity warring against your predetermined design for my life.

- I command order to replace all forms of disorder working against my life in the name of Jesus.

- Let gate openers and door openers begin to locate me today in the name of Jesus.

- Let those shooting at my destiny fall and die in the name of Jesus.

- Arise O God and cause all destiny frustraters to be destroyed.

- Cause my destiny helpers to be directed by the promptings of your Spirit and by divine revelation.

- Align me with those who will not only help me but will become a blessing to my family and entire bloodline.

- I declare that my foot will not be diverted, stalled nor will it slip off the path to destiny.

- Let the angels of the Lord hold me in their hands on the path to success to ensure that I don't dash my foot on a stumbling block.

- Destiny helpers arise and rush to my life now in the name of Jesus.

- Lord, I call them from the four corners of the earth and command that they reveal themselves in this season.

- Almighty God, let them come forth bringing gifts, opportunities, access, and levels of influence.

- Strengthen them in their callings O God and release your blessings over them continually.

- Bring them into your treasure rooms and cause them to be filled with your goodness.

- May the blessing of the Lord that makes rich and adds no sorrow to it be their portion continually in Jesus' name. Amen.

2.16 Seasons of Promotion

Scriptural Prayer Aids: Psalm 75:6, Esther 6:11, Daniel 2 :48, Luke 14 :11

- Father, I thank you that promotion does not come from the east or the west, but it comes from you.

- Let the anointing for promotion rest heavily upon me now in the name of Jesus.

- Cause all good and effectual doors to swing wide open on my behalf.

- Cause me to excel in my call and to walk in the power of my assignment continually.

- Great Judge you are the one who sets up one and dethrones another, cause me to be elevated in this season in Jesus' name.

- Loose the loins of kings on my behalf and make it impossible for my words to fall to the ground.

- Let men be unable to resist my requests and cause them to flourish without opposition all the days of my life.

- Cause me to be preferred above others in all forms of competition.

- Anoint me to excel above and beyond in my areas of calling and purpose.

- Anoint me with the fresh oil of promotion and cause the horn of elevation to remain strong in my life and bloodline.

- Father cause me to remain humble so that you can promote me in due season in Jesus' name.

- Father bring me into the realm of influence and cause me to sit with kings in Jesus' name.

- Father you are the one who lifts the poor out of the dust and the needy out of heaps, do the same for me.

- Raise me up O Lord so that I may walk and live in the elevated places of the earth.

- Let the glory of promotion rise on me this day in the name of Jesus.

- Lift my head my Lord and my God and cause the rule and authority you have given to me remain.

- Let supernatural advancement overtake every area of my life in the name of Jesus.

- Grant me divine speed in the area of promotion in the mighty name of Jesus.

- Let the areas where I am overlooked and disregarded become areas of tremendous blessing.

- Cause the mark of disfavour and disgrace to be completed wiped from my life.

- Father, I declare that my blessings will not be transferred to another in the mighty name of Jesus.

- Lord right now I access divine light that will begin to attract promotions to me.

- Cause nothing and no one contending for my promotion to gain any advantage over me.

- I declare that I wear a robe of favour and not garments of disgrace.

- I will have a good name in the earth all the days of my life and will never know disfavour.

- I will not lose my credibility and a good reputation will continually be a shield for me all my days.

- Let the power of advancement rest on my tongue as I speak life into my promotions let them swiftly manifest.

- Lord, please guard my promotions with your anointing.

- Make it impossible for my promotions to fail in Jesus' name.

- Give me the skills, insight, maturity, and spiritual direction to remain steadfast in my areas of promotion.

- Let honour and uprightness preserve me as you enlarge my coast.

- Enlarge my territory by the power of your right hand and reinforce my borders in the name of Jesus.

- May the territory I have gained in this season of promotion become legacy for my family and my generations in Jesus' name. Amen.

2.17 Ease in Progress

Scriptural Prayer Aids: Genesis 24:40 Psalm 119:105,
Isaiah 30:21, 1 Corinthians 16:9

- Almighty God, I ask that you guide me by your Holy Spirit.

- Cause me to walk having your word being a lamp to my feet and light to my path.

- Let no blockage or stumbling block come into my way in the name of Jesus.

- I ask that every restriction begin to break off my life and destiny.

- Today I step over every boundary the enemy has set for me in Jesus' name.

- I declare that by the power invested in me I will run through troops and leap over every high wall.

- I will command goodness and tender mercies in all areas of my life.

- Father, I declare that the loins of people of influence will be loosed on my behalf.

- Let no man be able to stand before me in opposition all the days of my life.

- I ask that you advance my cause in the earth by your right hand.

- With your holy hand and outstretched arm rush deliverance to every area of my life.

- Father, I come against demonic delay and detention of blessings and favour.

- Holy God, move swiftly on my behalf and cause those lusting after my goodness to fall in the trap of their own making.

- I declare that the gates into cities, countries and regions open on my behalf.

- Industries will bow and the mysteries into their innerworkings will be revealed.

- By divine revelation cause me to take territory wherever you have assigned me.

- Lord cause every demonic roadblock to crumble and fall in the name of Jesus.

- Help me to ride on the high places of the earth without hindrance in Jesus' name.

- Lord chart prosperous courses for me in every area of my life.

- Teach me how to lean and to depend on your direction.

- Father cause every wall of Jericho to become a heap before me.

- Cause the blessings that have been locked away from my family and bloodline to be released now.

- I cast out the spirit of barrenness in every area of my life in Jesus' name.

- I will ascend into places of promotion beyond my natural understanding and abilities in the name of Jesus.

- Father release strategic relationships and partnerships into my life.

- Break patterns of stagnation and self-sabotage from over me.

- I cast down imaginations that war against my progress in Jesus 'name.

- Let the wind of the Spirit begin to blow away man-made graves that have buried my potentials.

- Lord of the Harvest, cause me to reap in places that I have not sown in the mighty name of Jesus.

- Lord cause me to ascend in to greatness and to become a part-taker in overnight blessings.

- Expand my reach and grant me the anointing of enlargement.

- Let all good and effectual doors swing wide open for me in Jesus' name.

- Lord make me a blessing in this season in the mighty name of Jesus, amen.

2.18 The Blessing of a Thousand

Scriptural Prayer Aids: Deuteronomy 1:11, Genesis 49:25-26

- Father in the name of Jesus I ask that you cause me to walk in the blessings you intended for your Church.

- Father in blessing bless me and in multiplying, please multiply my efforts in the earth.

- Father may your blessing be released to me because I put my trust in you.

- Almighty God, bless me with favour and surround my life with it like a shield.

- Lord preempt my every move with blessings of goodness and place a crown of gold on my head.

- Lord, I declare that because I am blessed by you, I will inherit the earth.

- Abundantly bless me with your provision and satisfy me with your substance.

- Father command your blessing and let it overtake me in every area of my life.

- Almighty God may your blessing be so evident on my life that men will acknowledge it.

- Cause your blessing and favour to increase on my life in Jesus' name.

- Let everything about me announce and proclaim your blessing.

- Let the blessing of a thousand be over me and my household in Jesus' name.

- Bless me by the power of your right hand and the power o[f] glory.

- Cause your blessing to become a seal over me that cannot be broken.

- Let the season of blessing become permanent in every area of my life in Jesus' name, amen.

2.19 Alignment with Purpose & Destiny

Scriptural Prayer Aids: Ecclesiastes 3:1, Proverbs 16:3, Jeremiah 1:5

- Omnipotent God and All-Knowing Wonder I come to you today.
- Let there be light concerning my purpose and destiny in Jesus' name.
- I ask that you shine light on my talents and abilities and that you cause them to emerge.
- Let prophetic promptings be released to help me discover my true identity.
- Father break the power of all forms of deception and delusion warring against my purpose and destiny.
- Let everything about me be revealed by your Holy Spirit.
- Cause every destiny delay tactic to be destroyed by your fire.
- I declare that no demonic detention of my goodness will stand in the mighty name of Jesus.
- Let the unveiling of my purpose begin today in Jesus' name.
- Father, I come against evil diversions of my destiny and purpose.
- Lord bring me into the place of focus and help me to filter out distractions.
- I come against all forms of confusion and lack of clarity regarding my call.
- I refuse to be an aimless wanderer in the mighty name of Jesus.
- Let the veil be removed from my heart and mind concerning my destiny.
- Merciful Father, I cry out to you for light in Jesus' name.
- Grant me divine revelation about myself and expose the things about me that remain hidden.

- Let no lie that has been sown in my soul as a child prevail against my true call.
- Father give me an encounter with you that will set my life on the path to destiny.
- Almighty God silence every other voice vying for my attention and turn my focus solely to you.
- Cause every conspiracy formed against my destiny to be brought to nothing.
- Lord fight against those what war against my purpose in Jesus' name.
- Through you O God will ride upon the high places of purpose.
- The rest that comes with finding where I fit is mine in Jesus' name.
- I reject laziness and procrastination in the name of Jesus.
- Let my dreams no longer be fantasies but teach me how to put strategic effort into them.
- Father teach me the science of goal realization in the name of Jesus.
- Lord, I declare that I will rise above depression and self-pity in the mighty name of Jesus.
- I refuse to waste precious moments lamenting over passed failures.
- Teach me how to bounce back and to keep going after disappointment.
- Almighty God grant me courage to step out and do what you have placed in my heart.
- I arrest the spirit of fear and refuse to be tormented and crippled by it.
- Lord break the cycle of negativity and self-defeat off my life in Jesus' name.
- Arise O God and let every enemy that seeks to derail my purpose scatter.

- Let no destiny killer prosper, let their devices come to nothing in the mighty name of Jesus.
- Awake divine favour on my behalf as I walk out my purpose.
- Help me to pursue and to conquer in every area you have called me to serve.
- Righteous Judge, be glorified through the exploits I will undertake in this season in Jesus' name, amen.

2. 20 Spirits of Poverty & Financial Drought

Scriptural Prayer Aids: Job 5:15-16, Proverbs 13:8, Proverbs 22:7

- Father in the name of Jesus I ask that you teach my hands how to war and your fingers how to fight concerning my finances.

- Let every spirit of poverty lurking in any area of life be exposed and destroyed by fire.

- I arrest my association with poverty and break its power over my bloodline right now.

- Cause the sting of poverty to die in every area of my life in Jesus' name.

- Let this venom not be passed down to my children or grandchildren.

- Cause the foundation of poverty to be broken and destroyed.

- Father, I cast down every stronghold in my mind that keeps the spirit of poverty attached to me.

- I declare that I am not a candidate of financial drought in Jesus' name.

- Lord restore and replenish the avenues in which my financial resources have dried up.

- Let the wells of blessing connected to my finances to be unstopped in Jesus' name.

- I rebuke the effects of curses, spells, negative words, and evil altars warring against my finances.

- By the shed blood of the Lamb grant me divine exemption from ordinances setup against my prosperity.

- Father cause the heavens to be opened over the works of my hands and cause them to prosper.

- Rewrite the story of my financial life and cause it to become glorious in the mighty name of Jesus.

- Let every covenant made by my forefathers that has unleashed the spirit of poverty in my life to be revoked.

- Cancel the assignment of financial parasites and leaches out of my life.

- Let the virtue sucked out of my finances be restored a thousand-fold.

- I refuse to struggle to eat bread in the name of Jesus.

- I unmask and strip the spirit of poverty of its armour, let it become naked, bare, and disgraced, in Jesus' name.

- With the sword of the spirit, I cut off the head of the spirit of poverty.

- I cut through the damage it has done to my life and release fire on its unborn seed.

- I declare that the impact of poverty will never progress beyond this point in my life in Jesus' name.

- Lord give me the strategy to prevent a reoccurrence of financial drought in my life.

- Open my eyes to see where the enemy has made in-rows in my financial life.

- I declare that no bitter water will flow out of my finances.

- I declare that I will walk in financial favour every minute of day of the rest of my life.

- I declare that no desert spirit will ever attach itself again to my finances in Jesus' name.

- Let every spirit that has locked the heavens over my finances hand over the keys now.

- Cause the rivers and streams that have dried up in my financial life begin to flow again.

- Let the waters of the deep begin to break up and the dams of prosperity be broken for my sake.

- Flood my life with the blessing that makes rich, and which adds no sorrow to it.

- I declare that this will be the season where the former and latter rains will descend in my finances.

- Lord according to your will cause my prosperity to expand and multiply.

- By your hand of fire let the wells of wealth never be stopped up for all generations to come.

- Almighty God, I thank you that you are the one who plants men in prosperity, plant me O God and may I never be uprooted in Jesus' name amen.

2.21 Financial Slavery & Hardship

Scriptural Prayer Aids: I Kings 17:8-16, Matthew 6:26, Philippians 4:19

- Almighty God, let the spirit of slavery and everything it represents in my life be destroyed.

- Father turn my financial captivity into generational freedom in Jesus' name.

- I declare that the spirit of hardship will not have dominion over me.

- I refuse to live in the realm of hard labour, Lord create a way of escape for me.

- Father, I declare that my labour will never be in vain.

- Today I disassociate myself from profitless hard work in Jesus' name.

- Lord break the bonds of financial slavery from my life.

- Let the chains be broken by force and by fire in the name of Jesus.

- Arise O God for my help and hasten the destruction of every satanic oppression over my wealth.

- Make my way prosperous and shield me from economic turbulence.

- By your hand of fire clear the path for my financial success.

- Father let all forms of sorrow vanish from my labour.

- Let every ditch dug to bury my prosperity be destroyed.

- Wherever my wealth yielding ideas are buried let them be resurrected in Jesus' name.

- Lord, I cast down every evil altar erected for my downfall.

- Cause evil to slay every wicked spirit keeping me in a cycle of financial hardship n Jesus' name.

- Today and break myself free from all forms of financial captivity.

- As I walk out of slavery Father let the chains begin to break and let them be forever destroyed.

- Let the curse of a brassy heaven and an iron earth break from over my money.

- Today I declare that I have been set free by the power of your right hand in the name of Jesus, amen.

2.22 Spirits of Lack

Scriptural Prayer Aids: Deuteronomy 2 :7, Psalm 34:10, James 1:4, Proverbs 28 :27

- Father in the name of Jesus today by the power of your might I leave the territory of the land of not enough.

- Let your judgement fall on every spirit of lack preying on my goodness in Jesus' name.

- Let the season of insufficiency come to a perpetual end in my life.

- I declare that I will no longer live from paycheck to paycheck in Jesus' name.

- Let every parasite eating up my resources be exposed and be destroyed by fire.

- Let every thief and destroyer of my financial gains be destroyed by the might of your coming.

- Father cause every area of my life where my money is falling through the cracks be revealed.

- Lord reveal the streams of income you have for me that directly relate to my gifts and talents.

- Let the channels in my spirit be open and let me ascend into realms of divine revelation concerning my prosperity.

- Every ceiling that has been created in the realm of the spirit to limit and restrict my financial progress let them be shattered in the name of Jesus.

- Deliver me from the negative words I have consistently uttered over my financial future.

- I arrest everything the enemy is holding up against my prosperity and overrule them by the blood of Jesus.

- Let the tare in my finances be uprooted and burned to ashes in Jesus' name.

- When the enemy bends his bow to shoot his arrow at my financial resources let it be cut in pieces.

- I disassociate myself from economic downgrading and demise in Jesus' name.

- I declare that the pattern of eating crumbs breaks from off my family and bloodline today in Jesus' name.

- Lord, I thank you for your right hand of power that can elevate and transform my financial reality in Jesus' name, amen.

2.24 Financial Sabotage

Scriptural Prayer Aids: Job 1, Proverbs 20:23 , Luke 8:43

- I come against all forms of tragedy positioned to dry up my finances.

- Father, I declare that no sickness or disease will empty my pockets in Jesus' name.

- I arrest every spirit of trouble and torment coming up against my financial stability.

- Let the violent assault of the enemy on my money come to a perpetual end in the mighty name of Jesus.

- Let every evil whispering against my prosperity receive dumbness.

- Let no conspiracy against my business and other financial pursuits stand in the name of Jesus.

- Let all frustration at the edge of my financial breakthrough receive sudden destruction.

- Let persons sitting on my job promotion be removed in Jesus' name.

- Every counsel being raised up to block my prosperity receive perpetual destruction.

- Lord, search me and expose any tendencies and thought patterns that oppose my prosperity.

- Let my actions align with your desire and will for my wealth.

- Let every evil transaction conducted in the spirit realm over my money be disgraced and nullified in the name of Jesus.

- Father, I hide my wealth and my wealth yielding ideas under the blood of Jesus.

- Cause every ordinance set to bring me to financial ruin be wiped out by the power of the blood.

- Father shield my wealth from the destruction that prowls a midday.

- No matter how the strong the conspiracy is against my financial health it will be destroyed in the name of Jesus.

- Today, I crush every accusation of the enemy under my feet and declare myself financially free in Jesus' name, amen.

Financial Deliverance & Breakthrough

Scriptural Prayer Aids: Exodus 12:36, Psalm 105 :37, Isaiah 61:7

- Lord God of the breakthrough answer me by fire in the mighty name of Jesus.

- Today I push back at every high wall of partition between me and complete financial deliverance.

- Like the walls of Jericho let everything restricting my financial release receive the fate of utter destruction.

- I demand unconditional release from financial assault in the Jesus' name.

- God of Jeshurun ride on the heavens for my help concerning this matter.

- Be my strength and exceeding great reward in the name of Jesus.

- Let the mark of prosperity and progress be released and be written all over my life.

- Father give me the mantle for wealth and increase in the mighty name of Jesus.

- Reveal to me the central location for the manifestation of my wealth and increase.

- Plant me in the right business and right industry that will help me to thrive.

- Let the anointing to increase fall mightily on me right now.

- Cause the distance between me and my financial goals to be closed forever by the shed blood of the Lamb.

- Almighty God, bring swift deliverance to me concerning financial stagnancy.

- I command every spirit of backwardness and financial regression to be permanently cast out of my life in Jesus' name.

- Let every ritual performed with a snail or turtle, to cause my financial progress to be slowed and halted receive sudden and perpetual destruction.

- Turn the enemy's laughter against my progress into never-ending sorrow in the mighty name of Jesus.

- I declare that the breakthrough I have received in my finances will never be taken away in Jesus' name.

The Realm of Prosperity

Scriptural Prayer Aids: Deuteronomy 29:9, 1 Samuel 25:6, Job 36:11, Psalm 30:6

- Father let the realm of prosperity swing wide open for me this week in the name of Jesus.

- Let my wealthy place in the realm of the spirit be revealed and unlocked in the mighty name of Jesus.

- Let the wealth of the wicked laid up for the righteous begin to make its way to me.

- Cause the magnetic pull of the spirit begin to pull in the resources to guarantee my prosperity.

- Lord as I enter the realm of prosperity, I ask that you bed me down in the lush green pastures of financial increase.

- Keep me far from financial trouble and give me rest from everything that wars against my prosperity.

- By the power of the covenant let my place in this realm become secure.

- Lord reveal to me by your word how to remain prosperous in all seasons of life.

- Let my prosperity break out on every side and bring me into financial overflow.

- Father reveal the keys to my prosperity and teach me how to activate them.

- By your power and strength Almighty God increase my value and influence in the earth.

- Make me an ambassador of kingdom wealth for your glory.

- Let the doors of prosperity that I unlock in my lifetime never be closed for all my generations.

- Father teach me laws that govern this realm in the name of Jesus.

- I thank for the power of this dimension, now glorify yourself in life through it in Jesus' name, amen.

Generational Wealth

Scriptural Prayer Aids: Deuteronomy 8:18, Deuteronomy 28 :12, Proverbs 13:22

- Father in the name of Jesus I ask that you bring me into alignment with the generational plan you have for my life.

- Position me for generational wealth in the mighty name of Jesus.

- Let the financial breaches that have manifested from the lives of my forefathers be closed by the blood of the Lamb.

- I declare that the spirit of poverty will not latch onto another generation in the name of Jesus.

- Let every spell, incantation, evil decree, and pronouncement over my generational blessings be destroyed.

- I declare that the judgement written must fall on all evil designs and intentions concerning the prosperity of my generations.

- I declare that the children in my bloodline will possess the gates of prosperity and abundance in Jesus 'name.

- They will become mighty in the earth regarding the acquisition and deployment of wealth.

- They will become like arrows in the quiver of the Lord and will be shot into directions that will advance the prosperity of the kingdom.

- Father according to your divine will let the anointing to excel fall upon my bloodline.

- Way-making God make a way of prosperity for my bloodline where men say there is no way.

- Let the channels in the heavens be opened and let it begin to rain down new possibilities for my generations.

- Cause the anointing for wealth acquisition and maintenance to begin to manifest now.

- Father let your word become a light to my path and a light to my feet for prosperity in all generations in Jesus' name.

2.28 Undiagnosed Sicknesses & Diseases
Scriptural Prayer Aids: Exodus 23:25, Jeremiah 33:6, I Peter 2 :24

- Omniscient God I call on you now in Jesus' name.

- Lord you made my body and every system in it.

- I ask Father that you expose and destroy every stranger lurking around in my body.

- I intercept the arrows of the enemy being shot at my health.

- Let sickness and disease be uprooted out of their illegal.

- With your spirit in me, which is your lamp, search out every organ, ligament, tissue, and cell.

- I pray that by divine revelation you expose everything hiding in my body.

- Let light shine in every dark area and call these sicknesses and diseases by their name and nature.

- As they are called out let them be permanently cast out in Jesus' name.

- Let all unexplainable pains, discomforts and feelings of unease vanish from my body.

- By the shed blood of the Lamb let every evil plantation in my body receive sudden destruction.

- Cause every incision made in my body through evil initiations to sealed up by the blood.

- Let every poison in my environment be neutralized by the blood of Jesus.

- Sun of Righteousness with healing in your wings rise on my behalf and break the back of the oppressor in the name of Jesus.

- Almighty God, make me completely whole and let nothing that the enemy has done concerning my health become a pattern in my life.

- According to your tender mercies and lovingkindness let it be done in Jesus' name, amen.

2.29 Seasonal Sicknesses

Scriptural Prayer Aids: Psalm 41:3, Deuteronomy 32 :39,   Isaiah 41:10

- Father, you have declared that the sun should not strike me by day or the moon by night.

- I declare that no ordinance made with consultation with the sun, moon and stars will have dominion over me.

- Lord, you have commanded that I should subdue the earth and according to your word, I take jurisdiction over my space.

- Let nothing in the air, on land or in the sea affect my body in Jesus' name.

- Father let sicknesses that wait to strike me at night receive sudden destruction.

- Cause no night raider to attack my body as I sleep in Jesus' name.

- Let the eaters of flesh and drinkers of blood be cut off in Jesus' name.

- Uproot them out of the places where they lurk and let their habitation become desolate.

- Almighty God, destroy hunters of the night that seek to harm my body.

- Become a shield and defense against time sensitive sickness and diseases.

- Let there be no transfer of sickness and disease through family members, friends, associates, or frequent environments.

- I renounce every sickness and disease raised up in my bloodline to attack me at a particular age in Jesus' name.

- By the power of your might release me from the fear of changing seasons.

- I come against unusual hormonal shifts based on lunar activities.

- Bring creation into alignment with my person, purpose, and destiny.

- Father, I thank you for demonstrating your power and might concerning this matter in Jesus' name, amen.

2.30 Genetic Weaknesses

Scriptural Prayer Aids: Exodus 34:7, Proverbs 26:2, Galatians 3:13

- Elohim, Creator-God I come to you today in the name of Jesus.

- I ask that you visit the foundation of my bloodline and that you will begin to purge it in Jesus' name.

- I confess that because of the shed blood of the Lamb I have been regenerated in Christ Jesus.

- Let my DNA and gene pool be made whole now by the blood of Jesus.

- By the power of the resurrection, let every cell, molecule, tissue, and organ receive strength and renewed life.

- Father let generational sicknesses and diseases be flushed out of my blood line.

- Visit the foundation of my family tree and destroy everything existing there that you did not plant.

- Let every misfiring, miscommunication, and misalignment in my organs be reversed in Jesus' name.

- Let every deficiency I was born with be rectified by the blood of the Lamb.

- Father regulate the systems in my body by the word of your power.

- Cause every genetic abnormality transferred in my life from the womb to be reversed.

- Counter every attack on my organs through my DNA with your presence.

- Break me free of childhood sicknesses and diseases still manifesting in my body.

- I command my organs to stop obeying the voice of strangers and to become subjected to the voice of God and his authority only.

- Let every enemy waging war against my purpose and destiny through my body be utterly destroyed.

- O Lord fight against them that fight against me and trouble those that trouble me.

- Cause me to prevail and to overcome in the mighty name of Jesus' amen.

2.31 Degenerative Diseases

Scriptural Prayer Aids: Genesis 27:1, 1 Samuel 4:15, John 9:1-3,

- Almighty God I arrest mental and physical decline in old age.

- I come against Dementia and Alzheimer's in Jesus' name.

- Father cause my strength and faculties to remain strong even as I age.

- Lord renew my strength and youth like the eagle and deliver me from the ravishes of time.

- Almighty God, let not the dictates of time and space prevail against my health in Jesus' name.

- I arrest demonic memory loss and the loss of mobility.

- I declare that my eyes will not get dim, nor will my faculty fail for all the days of my life.

- Let every attack on my brain and my brain cells be countered with the blood of Jesus.

- Cause every damage done to my body because of lifestyle habits be reversed.

- Father command your lovingkindness and tender mercies in every stage of my life.

- Faithful God as you have declared that you will never leave or forsake me cause it to manifest in every stage of my life.

- Holy Father appoint days of blessing and peace over my body in Jesus' name.

- Make me to know the wisdom and favour of old age.

- Let my latter days become far greater than my former days in Jesus' name.

- I come against blindness, deafness, and dumbness in Jesus' name.

- I declare that I will not lose any of my senses nor will they become weakened as I age in Jesus' name.

- I declare that none of my organs will fail and that none of my bodily systems will malfunction or decline.

- Father, I thank you that you are my shield and defense and my exceeding great reward in Jesus' name, amen.

2.32 Deformities & Paralysis

Scriptural Prayer Aids: Matt. 15: 30-31, Acts 3:2, Acts 14:8

- Father let every abnormality in my bone structure be reversed now.

- Let the weaknesses in my limbs receive strength in Jesus' name.

- Let every disease that leads to deformities be healed.

- Cause everything that desires to change the God-ordained structure of my body to receive sudden destruction.

- I prophesy to any dry bone manifesting in my body and command that they come back to life.

- Let every arrow of paralysis be reversed and cut in pieces in Jesus' name.

- I command every legality set against my life and bloodline that causes birth defects to be annihilated.

- Father step down in my DNA and gene pool as a mighty man of war and scatter everything coming down my bloodline that will lead to paralysis and deformity.

- Father, I come against freak accidents and vehicular accidents in the name of Jesus.

- I arrest the spirit of tragedy and the violent assault of the wicked one against my health.

- I declare that I will not be a candidate of the spirit of Amalek that catches its victims off guard.

- Let no conspiracy against by body stand in the mighty name of Jesus.

- Let no misdiagnosis and/or wrong medication lead to any form of paralysis in my life.

- Father, I declare that I will not lose any of my limbs in Jesus' name.

- I declare that none of my bones will be broken in Jesus' name.

- As I came into the world physically whole so I will depart in the mighty name of Jesus.

- Father, I declare that my entire being will rejoice before and will be at rest in Jesus' name, amen.

2.33 Healing & Creative Miracles

Scriptural Prayer Aids: Matthew 8: 5-13, Luke 7: 11-18 , John 2: 1-11, John 4:46-50

- Father release me into the realm of healing and creative miracles.

- Let your healing virtue be released from the crown of my head to the souls of my feet.

- Heal me O God and I will be healed save me and I will be saved.

- Almighty God let your creative power begin to manifest in my life.

- By the power of your might let the heavens open over my head.

- Cause the tangible weight of your presence to fill the atmosphere.

- Let there be a shift ordered in the heavens over my body in Jesus' name.

- Cause me to tap into the wells of healing and deliverance right now.

- By your shed blood let my cells, molecules, organs, tissues, and ligaments come into order.

- Father deliver me on a molecular, cellular, and systemic level in Jesus' name.

- Structural, systemic, and metabolic damage be reversed now in Jesus' name.

- Damaged and missing organs be replaced now in the mighty name of Jesus.

- Let malfunctioning systems be replaced now in the mighty name of Jesus.

- Father cause missing limbs to begin to grow back now in Jesus' name.

- As my cells breathe in the power of your glory let transformation take place over my entire body.

- Cause Edenic glory to return to by physical body and let my anatomy become a wonder of modern science in Jesus' name.

- Lord, I thank you for doing exceeding, abundantly and far above anything I could think or ask, in Jesus' name, amen.

PART III
THE FAMILY

God instituted the family out of his good counsel. The first family was created in the Garden of Eden. He protected His creation and provided for them. God will do the same for your family. Leave no stone unturned when you pray over your family and everything that defies God's design for it must give way.

3.1 The Dominion of Adam

Scriptural Prayer Aids: Genesis 1:26-28, Genesis 9: 1-3, Psalm 8:4-6

Petition:

- Father in the name of Jesus I declare that as man I am born to lead and to demonstrate your glory in the earth.

- I arrest every agent of satan which desires to abort this reality.

- My gender role will not be contaminated, violated, or reversed in Jesus' name.

- As the head of my household Lord teach me how to become a priest after your order.

- Grant me revelation concerning how to rightly divide the word of truth to my family.

- Let your word never depart from my bloodline for all generations unborn to time.

- Father, release your agenda and blueprint for my family and teach me how to effectively bring it to pass.

- Open my spiritual eyes and give me vision; let the entrance of your word bring me light.

- Lord, I surrender every life experience that has sought to minimize the call on my life.

- Today, let they yoke-destroying power of your spirit begin to break me loose from all bondage in Jesus' name.

- Give me the boldness I need to come into all you have predetermined and predesigned for me.

- Show me how to subdue and conquer the earth.

- Cause me to become mighty upon on the earth so I can establish your agenda in it.

- Let the anointing of the sons of Issachar fall mightily on me so I will know what to do in the times I live in.

- O Lord bless me and enlarge my territory by your mighty hand.

- Release wisdom, knowledge and understanding I have never known.

- Let my words drop as dew and let my counsel shine as the noonday sun.

- Give me an understanding heart and grant me favour with all men.

- Launch me into the realm of prosperity and let nothing cause my assignment as provider to be diminished.

- Father make my name great and let it continue as long as the sun.

- Bring me into the dimension of influence and cause me to ride upon the high places of the earth.

- Lord crown me with lovingkindness and establish my doings in the name of Jesus.

- Plead my cause in the earth and position me to prosper by the power of your right hand.

- Lord make me a mighty spiritual warrior; teach my hands how to war and my fingers how to fight in Jesus 'name.

- Father give me supernatural advancement in this season of my life.

- Let the anointing for divine acceleration fall mightily on me.

- Release me into overnight blessings and let there be a sudden shift into goodness in all that concerns me.

- Today Father I draw on your supernatural strength to accomplish your will for my life.

- Empower me through your omnipotence and make the impossible possible for me this week.

- Create plain paths for my feet and by your power I will tread down all my enemies in Jesus' name.

- Lord, I thank you for your plans and purposes for my life and declare that they will not fail in Jesus' name, amen.

3.2 The Dominion of Eve

Scriptural Prayer Aids: *Genesis 1:26-28, Genesis 2:21-23, Genesis 3:15*

- Father let the dominion you have given me come into full manifestation in Jesus' name.

- Let the glory that Eve had before the fall be my portion in this season of my life.

- Align everything about my life according to your will and purpose.

- Let your glory fall mightily upon me and anoint me the with oil of virtue.

- Grant me overwhelming and unconventional favour.

- Increase me in favour with you with favour with all men.

- Let the assignment of my womanhood become manifested mightily in my life.

- Cause me to find favour with all the people I encounter.

- I declare that my assignment will never be diluted, perverted, or aborted.

- Father cause me to become fruitful and to multiply in all areas of my life.

- Teach me how to harness the power of submission and to live according to your divine order.

- Loose the loins of kings and queens on my behalf and cause me to possess the treasures of darkness.

- Teach me how to be a mother of children, (both physical and spiritual) and of the outcome of visions and destinies.

- Almighty God, none that you place in my hands will be lost or will become underdeveloped and malnourished in Jesus' name.

- Make me a help meet for your agenda in the earth so shall I prosper and be established.

- Let my words become like dew upon the earth and let my presence change the atmosphere around me by your glory.

- Teach me how to establish and sustain legacy over generations in the name of Jesus.

- Let your perfect will be done in all areas of my life in Jesus' name, amen.

3.3 Spouses

Scriptural Prayer Aids: Esther 1:20, Eph. 5:25, Col. 3:18-19

Petition:

- Holy God, I thank you that marriage is honourable and the bed is undefiled in all.

- Almighty God, you are the one who ordained marriage and so I place my marriage in your hands.

- Lord let not wrath and resentment take root in my marriage.

- Cause your peace to take up residence in my marriage.

- Cause the blessings which come with making this covenant become our reality.

- Lord, please strengthen our commitment to each other.

- Teach us how to show mercy one to the other.

- Hide our marriage under the shadow of your wings, in the name of Jesus.

- Father what you have joined together let no emotional problem, family problem, and financial problem separate.

- Cause your peace to overshadow our marriage.

- I plead the blood of Jesus over our home, children, finances and destinies, in the name of Jesus.

- Lord cause the works of our hands to prosper in the name of Jesus.

- Help us to prevail in our prayer lives in the name of Jesus.

- Let your kingdom come in our lives and manifest without measure.

Husbands

- Father help me, as a husband, to love my wife even as Christ loves the Church.

- Help me to be a priest in my house, so that I may lead my family to the place of prayer and praise, in the name of Jesus.

- Give me vision, so that I may lead my family into the fullness of what you intended for us, from the foundation of the world.

- Teach me to be patient, kind and gentle with my wife because she is the weaker vessel, in the name of Jesus.

- Father, cause her to find safety, comfort and affirmation in my words and actions.

- Help me to build up my wife and children, so that they may become all that you have called them to be.

Wives

- Lord, help me to respect and honour my husband in my words and actions.

- Show me how to truly submit to my husband's leadership, in the name of Jesus.

- Cause my husband and children to rise up and call me blessed.

- Teach me how to become a good advisor to my husband and children.

- Let my words bring life and sustenance to my husband and children.

- Father, teach me how to effectively minister to my husband.

- Glorify yourself in our lives in the name of the Lord Jesus. Amen.

3.4 Home

Scriptural Prayer Aids: I Sam. 25:5-6, Psalm 91:10, Isaiah
  32:18

Petition:

- Almighty God, I dedicate my home to you in the name of
  Jesus.

- Lord please make it your resting place.

- Father, I uproot every demonic plantation on my property,
  in the name of Jesus.

- Let every satanic ritual or covenant performed, on the
  land surrounding my house or inside my house, be
  rendered null and void.

- Let your kingdom come in my residence and cause your
  angels to have free access to my home.

- Cause them to become a shield against demonic activity
  in my home.

- Father, let every plot and plan of the wicked one, to
  disrupt my home, receive double destruction, in the name
  of Jesus.

- Cause your wall of fire to be around my residence.

- Let all demonic spies who are seeking to break in and
  destroy my home, be thrown into perpetual confusion.

- Let the mark of the blood of Jesus become a
  border of protection around my house.

- Father, I declare that no plague shall come near my
  dwelling, in the name of Jesus.

- The pestilence which walks in darkness, shall not
  take up residence in my home, in the name of Jesus.

- Almighty God, cause your glory to cover my home, in the
  name of Jesus.

- Let my home become a beacon of change in my community.

- Let your peace which passes all understanding reside in it.

- Help me to discern the presence of angels in my home and to be receptive, to the messages they have to deliver.

- Let no demonic agent contend with my angel of blessing, in the name of Jesus.

- Cause my home to become a light for those who grope in darkness.

- Let every feeling of selfishness and arrogance that I may harbour concerning my home die, in the name of Jesus.

- I declare that my household shall be saved, in the name of Jesus.

- I declare that no evil altar will be raised up in my home.

- Almighty God, help me not to entertain any kind or form of idolatry, in my residence.

- Lord let my home become your temple.

- Cause everything that I do behind closed doors, to bring you honour and praise.

- Father, I come against every activity of maliciousness, which will cause me to be at war with my neighbours.

- Make my life a witness to those whom I live amongst, in the name of Jesus.

- Make my home a place of refuge for the outcast and the down trodden.

- Father, I drive out every form of hostility and confusion out of my house, in the name of Jesus.

- I declare that my house will never become a den for robbery and perversion.

- Lord, help me to set a watch over the things I entertain in my home, in Jesus' name.

- Let nothing defile my dwelling in the name of Jesus.

- Almighty God, I thank you for preserving my home from evil. Amen.

3.5 Parents

Scriptural Prayer Aids: 2 Corinth. 12:14, Eph. 6:4, I Timothy 5:8

> *Petition:*

- Father, grant me the wisdom to raise my child/children in the name of Jesus.

- Make my life an example for him/her/them to follow in the name of Jesus.

- Father, help me to always pray for my child/children.

- I dedicate myself to teaching my children your word.

- Show me how to train him/her/them up in the way he/she/they ought to go.

- Father, I release your blessing over my child/children in the name of Jesus.

- I break the power of any negative word, I have spoken over him/ her /them, in the name of Jesus.

- Help me to guide him/her/them on the path to destiny, in the name of Jesus.

- Help me to lead him/her/them with patience and understanding.

- Help me not to neglect my child/children because of work or ministry.

- Help me to correct him/her/them in love when they are wrong.

- Make me a pursuer and manifestation of your peace.

- Let my home become a haven for my child/children in the name of Jesus.

- Holy One, let everything in my environment, that is hostile to their growth and development begin to give way.

- Lord, I come against offence and bitterness in my relationship with my child/children.

- Father, let unforgiveness and revenge not find a place in my relationship with my child/children.

- Lord, let nothing that I have said or done consciously or subconsciously, bring a divide between me and my child/children.

- I declare that I shall not lose my child/children to prostitution, gang violence, drugs, sexual perversion, the occult or the lusts of this world.

- Turn my heart towards my child/children so that his/her/their heart/s will be turned towards me.

- I resurrect my family altar in the name of Jesus.

- Let my home be called a place of prayer in the name of Jesus.

- Lord, rid me of the tendency to dominate and manipulate my child/ children.

- Help me to recognize that you have given them to me as gifts which must be protected and cared for.

- Father, help me to create an environment of trust and acceptance for my child/children.

- I repent if I have knowingly or unknowingly abused my child/ children in any way.

- Father, let my child/children feel the love of God flowing from my heart towards him/her/them, in the name of Jesus.

- Lord, let my words be filled with encouragement and kindness toward my child/children.

- Lord, I break every curse that I have knowingly or unknowingly released over my child/children.

- Let your life and presence fill my home, in the name of Jesus.

- Thank you Lord, for teaching me how to parent in these troublesome times. Amen.

3.6 Children

Scriptural Prayer Aids: Genesis 22:17, Psalm 144:12, Acts 2:17, Col. 3:20

Petition:

- Father, in the name of Jesus, deliver my child/children from evil and from the clutches of darkness.

- Father, deliver my young one/s from the snare of the fowler, in the name of Jesus.

- I plead the blood of Jesus against the spirit of suicide and I command it to be consumed, by the fire of the living God, in the name of Jesus.

- Spirit of the living God, stand upright within my child/children, in the name of Jesus.

- I plead the blood of Jesus over his/her/their mind/s in the name of Jesus.

- Sanctify his/her/their mind/s in the name of Jesus.

- Grant onto him/her/them holy appetites, in the name of Jesus.

- Cause him/her/ them to hunger and thirst after righteousness.

- Let your name be magnified through him/her/them in the name of Jesus.

- Holy One, cause him/her/them to know you as their shield and defence.

- Lord of Hosts, cause him/her/them to know you as their invincible armour.

- Father in the name of Jesus; make his/her/their feet like hind's feet that he/she/they may walk upon high places.

- I decree that he/she/they will not die but live to declare the glory of the Lord, in the land of the living.

- Loose the bands of wickedness in his/her/their school/s, in the name of Jesus.

- I command the back of every oppressive spirit raised up against him/ her/them, to be broken, in the name of Jesus.

- Grant unto him/her/them godly wisdom beyond his/her/their years.

- Make him/her/them of quick understanding in the fear of the Lord, in the name of Jesus Christ.

- Teach him/her/them how to wage an effective warfare through your name.

- I bind the spirit of pride in the name of Jesus Christ.

- Let humility abound in him/her/them in Jesus' name.

- I bind the spirit of rebellion in the name of Jesus.

- Cause them to be obedient to your will, in the name of Jesus.

- Father, you are a man of war, fight for my child/children, in the name of Jesus.

- Sanctify him/her/them unto good works.

- Let his/her/their heart/s be filled with love in the name of Jesus.

- May the peace of God rest bountifully upon him/her/them, in the name of Jesus.

- I declare that he/she/they will not be deceived by the enemy, in the name of Jesus.

- Father fill him/her/them up with your truth.

- Bless him/her/them abundantly.

- Uproot every negative word sown into his/her/their spirit/s, in the name of Jesus.

- I come against tragedy and untimely death in the name of Jesus.

- Father, make him/her/them a force to be reckoned with in the earth.

- I declare that he/she/they shall possess the gates of the enemy.
- Let the glory that you will give him/her/them in this season, never be taken away, in Jesus' name. Amen.

3.7 Bloodline -*(lineage, generation)* **Scriptural Prayer Aids**:

Psalm 37:22, Prov. 3:33, Titus 3:5 ***Petition:***

- The God who keeps covenant to a thousand generations, hear me for thy name's sake.

- Father, please turn towards me with favour and grant me this request in the name of Jesus.

- Never let your tender mercies and loving kindness depart from my bloodline, in the name of Jesus.

- Give me an inheritance of supernatural power and influence, in the name of Jesus.

- Cause me to store up spiritual wealth for my children's children.

- Preserve my bloodline from evil, in the name of Jesus Christ.

- I pronounce the blessings of fruitfulness, brilliance, excellence, health and prosperity over my bloodline.

- Give me the birthright of the wise and prudent, in the name of Jesus.

- Cause righteousness to flourish through my generation.

- As of this day, my bloodline will know no more lack, in the name of Jesus.

- Let your word never depart from my lips nor from the lips of my descendants.

- Bring me into the inheritance you have ordained for me, from before the foundations of the world.

- Cause my sons and daughters to accomplish far more, than I ever will, in the name of Jesus.

- Cause the anointing to continually flow over my bloodline.

- Let every root of iniquity dry up from my bloodline, in the name of Jesus.

- Lord, cause the blessing of a thousand to be released over my bloodline.

- Lord, I release length of days over my bloodline, in the name of Jesus.

- I arrest every irregularity in my gene pool, in the name of Jesus.

- I arrest and cast out every mental and emotional dysfunction from my bloodline.

- I break every cycle of negative tendencies and behaviour from my bloodline in the name of Jesus.

- I declare that the days which my generation experiences, will be as the days of heaven on earth.

- May the legacy of kingdom dominion be ever present in my bloodline.

- Let every demonic force that has positioned itself, with the intent of destroying the goodness in my bloodline, receive double destruction.

- Let every form of limitation break from off of my bloodline.

- Father, let the knowledge of your glory, be the portion of my bloodline, in the name of Jesus.

- Father, I speak into the generations which are to come and I declare, that the favour of God will rest upon them, as long as time lasts.

- Thank you for hearing and answering prayers, in Jesus' name. Amen.

3.8 Evil Family Patterns

Scriptural Prayer Aids: Genesis 20:1-13, Genesis 26:6-7, Genesis 25:29-34, 27:18-22, Genesis 34:13-29, 37:31-34

- Almighty God, visit the foundation of my family and cleanse it by the power of the blood.

- Arise O God and let familiar spirits be scattered and let them never be reinforced in my bloodline.

- Let tragedies my great-grandfather, grandfather and father experienced never raise their heads in my life.

- I declare that every serpent will be crushed under my feet.

- Let the fire of God destroy every demonic altar erected in the foundation of my family.

- Cause every evil precedence established by anyone in my family to be uprooted in Jesus' name.

- Spiritual battles coming down my bloodline be brought to nothing in Jesus' name.

- Lord help me to overcome every negative arrow positioned against my family.

- Let the arrows of the wicked return to their own bosoms.

- Cause no negative word spoken against my family and my progress stand.

- Arise O God and dismantle evil ordinances set in my place of birth.

- Now may my head be lifted above my enemies in Jesus' name.

- Break every iron-like curse and yoke manifesting in my family.

- Bind up the hand of the enemy and cause his plans to be perpetually frustrated.

- Shake the foundations of evil consultations concerning the welfare of my family.

- Lord sever every tie that holds us bound to spells, incantations, and witchcraft curses.

- Let the pattern of your perfect will overrule and overturn every negative and demonic pattern set up against us.

- Lord through divine favour let me be the first among those to rise in my family in Jesus' name, amen.

PART IV
DELIVERANCE

Deliverance is a process that brings freedom, prepares a way of escape, initiates help, and enables us to experience victory and liberty. Every Christian is indeed saved having walked through the born-again experience. However, the work of salvation is an ongoing process. Our spirits are immediately saved but our souls go through continuous stages of redemption and our bodies will be renewed when we are glorified at Christ's return. Our souls carry our intellect, will, self-consciousness, personality, and emotions. It is here that we have most of the contentions in our Christian walk, and this is the place from which the enemy attempts to take over our lives.

Deliverance comes to us in three levels, there is deliverance that we must go through to rid ourselves of demonic oppression as well as thought patterns, habits and emotional states that are ungodly. The next level is being delivered into the dimension of freedom, breakthrough, prosperity, and healing. The third level is for the Believer to deliver up what God has deposited in him from the foundations of the world.

We must come into the glory of deliverance if we are going to manifest the full measure of who we are in Christ. Expressing a need for deliverance is nothing to be ashamed of because every deliverance experience is designed to bring us into newness life as well as greater levels of power and authority with God.

The Need for Deliverance after Salvation

We are saved but live in a fallen word. We have been contaminated by the systems of this world and have a sin nature. Our carnal nature is ever at war with your spiritual nature. Our carnal nature craves after and delights in sin and is at odds with God. Our spiritual man desires spiritual things and yearns after the things that please God (Romans 8:7-10).

A need for deliverance therefore stems from the mere fact that we are living in a fallen world. We must interface with a world that is designed to pull us away from God and to draw us back into a life of sin. Added to this is the fact that many of us have indulged in sinful activities which opened doors to the enemy before we got saved. Others of us are coming out of backgrounds where witchcraft was readily practiced, have had our placenta manipulated, are recipients of the consequences of ancestral evil, believe in astrology (the horoscope, zodiac signs), participated in demonic rituals, have been exposed to demonic initiations, are walking under generational curses, and have had our homes and personal properties dedicated to satan.

All these realities underscore the need for deliverance and speak its relevance in present-day Christianity.

4.1 Destructive Cycles & Patterns

Scriptural Prayer Aids: Numbers 32:13, Judges 14-16, Luke 8:43-48

- Lord of Hosts, deliver me from negative and destructive cycles.

- Seasons of destruction that are time sensitive and occur in specific days, months and years be wiped out of my life by the blood of Jesus.

- The enemy comes to kill, steal, and destroy but you have come that I may have life in abundance.

- Cycles of death and hell I command you to be destroyed now in Jesus' name.

- I declare that the pattern of untimely death is permanently broken off my life.

- I speak against freak accidents and vehicular accidents and declare that they will not manifest in my life.

- Patterns of generational diseases loose your hold over me now in Jesus' name.

- Deformities, paralysis, incurable diseases be uprooted from my bloodline by force and by fire.

- I resist predictions of major surgeries that have plagued my family line in Jesus' name.

- Cycles of poverty I command you to break now in the name of Jesus.

- Father let the cycle of drought end from over my finances.

- I declare that the spirit of financial struggle will not be transferred to me in the name of Jesus.

- I will not eat bread out of desolate places nor will my children become beggars.

- Cycles of unhealthy and abusive relationships I arrest you now in Jesus' name.

- Father expose and weed out every imposter in my life.

- Deliver me from the residue of past relationships that keep me attracting the wrong people.

- Let automatic failure in my relationships be cancelled now in Jesus' name.

- Lorddelivermefromthoughtpatternsandtendenciesthatkeep negativityaliveinmylife.

- I cancel the effect of negative words I have spoken over myself, let them not contaminate my destiny.

- By the shed blood of the Lamb I declare divine exemption from every negative thing in my environment.

- Let the blood of Jesus permanently wipe out the ordinances of any damage done to my purpose and destiny.

- According to your lovingkindness launch me into your cycle of blessing and advancement.

- Father bed me down in lush green pastures and cause me to find rest beside still waters in Jesus' name, amen.

4.2 Demonic Covenants

Scriptural Prayer Aids: Psalm 83, 2 Samuel 15: 12-15, Ezekiel 22:25

- Father, today I stand on the tenets of the power of the surpassing covenant of Jesus Christ.

- I declare that through the superior blood of the Lamb I overcome the devil and his agents.

- I declare that no demonic covenant made concerning me will stand.

- Father let every evil altar raised up against my life and family be dismantled by fire.

- Let no offering that my forefathers have initiated to idols will not be held against me the spirit realm.

- I declare divine exemption from the effects every curse associated with idol worship.

- I declare the blood of goats and chicken will never speak better things than the superior blood of the Lamb.

- Lord cause your blood to prevail and to become a defense against all the accusations of the enemy.

- Let no let legality keep me bound to the penalties of my forefathers.

- Almighty God, visit the foundation of my life and breakup everything planted there that is a result of a demonic covenant.

- Let every stronghold positioned against my progress and wellbeing because of covenant be broken.

- Cause the surpassing power of your divine covenant concerning me to overturn and overrule ungodly inferior covenants.

- By the strength of the covenant let evil be rooted out and destroyed out of its hiding places in my life.

- Let hindering spirits lose their legal positions of power and authority over my life and bloodline.

- Cause all doors opened by demonic covenants to be closed forever by the power of your right hand in Jesus' name.

- According to your lovingkindness and tender mercies blot out all ordinances written against my life in Jesus' name, amen.

Familiar & Monitoring Spirits

Scriptural Prayer Aids: Leviticus 19:31, Deuteronomy 18 : 10-12, 2 Kings 21:1-6

- Father blind the eyes of monitoring spirits and send them into utter confusion.

- Those who are seeking information about life by looking through crystal balls and the hiring of mediums will receive complete madness and desolation.

- Let no evil eye have dominion over me or my family.

- Cause the power of familiar spirits to be broken off my life now in the name of Jesus.

- Arise O Lord and perpetually disgrace the whisperings of wicked spirits.

- I declare that the conspiracies being hatched against me will come to nothing.

- I decree that the desires and designs of satan will be aborted over my life.

- Let spirits conducting spiritual surveillance on my life have their eyes plucked out and destroyed.

- Father, I declare that no gossiper will take root in my life.

- Lord teach me how to keep silent and to move strategically in every area of my life.

- Let no study or investigation of my life patterns be used against me by familiar spirits.

- Father let your judgment fall on lines of communication between spiritual saboteurs and abortionists.

- Cause their plans and purposes to be aborted in Jesus' name.

- Father scatter every gathering called for my downfall in the name of Jesus.

- Father, I declare that when they take counsel together, it will come to nothing.

- When they speak the word it shall not stand because you are with me.

- The enemies may surround me like bees but in the name of the Lord, I will destroy them.

- Let the whirlwind target their dwellings and let their habitations become desolate.

- Lord expose and disgrace familiar spirits masquerading as dead family members in Jesus' name.

- I declare that my mind and spirit will not be intercepted or breached by familiar spirits while I sleep.

- I will have no conversation or take counsel from any but the spirit but the Spirit of the living God.

- As of today, no monitoring spirit will block, frustrate, or stop my progress in Jesus' name.

Tormenting Spirits

Scriptural Prayer Aids: 1 Samuel 16:14-16, Matthew 15:22, Matthew 17:15

- Father in the name of Jesus I ask that you take control of my mind.

- I plead the blood of Jesus over my thought patterns and mindset in Jesus' name.

- I refuse to allow the trauma of my past to become a hunter of my future and parasite to my present.

- I declare that no negative spirit that has become resident in my family will have dominion over my life.

- Father deliver me from thoughts and ideas that keep me in fear and un belief.

- Almighty God help me to gird up the loins of my mind and to keep on the helmet of salvation.

- Almighty God, I cast down ordinances that cause time-sensitive mental attacks.

- I reject mental downward spirals that trigger negative attitudes, behaviours and turmoil.

- I refuse to live a life dominated by emotions and declare that I will be led by the Spirit in Jesus' name.

- I rebuke the spirit of fear and its crippling effects on every area of my life.

- Lord today I raise up the shield of faith against the fiery darts of the enemy sand declare that they will be quenched.

- I declare that my mind is sheltered under the wings of God.

- I confess that I possess perfect peace because my mind is consistently on my Lord and saviour.

- Spirits of mental paralysis and depression loose your hold over my mind and emotions.

- Father deliver me from night fears, nightmares, and demonic assaults in the dream.

- I come against seasonal depression and lingering emotional pain.

- Today I overcome by the blood the Lamb and the word of my testimony in Jesus' name.

Spells & Incantations

Scriptural Prayer Aids : Isaiah 8 : 19, Isaiah 47 :9, Ezek. 13:18

- Lord of Hosts I ask you to go before me as a shield in the name of Jesus.
- I draw a line with the blood of Jesus around my life and family and declare that no spell or incantation concerning us will stand.
- By the superior blood of the Lamb let every demonic threat against my life and livelihood be dismantled by fire.
- Let the tongues of those establishing demonic ordinances with their words against me cleave to the roof of their mouths.
- Cast down high looks and bring evil manipulators of the spirit realm to open disgrace.
- Let your anger be stirred up against those who release the agenda of sorcery in my life.
- Father you are a witness against sorcerers let their devices refuse to perform and backfire in Jesus' name.
- Father break the teeth of wicked in their mouths and bring them into perpetual silence.
- As they love cursing, let it cover their dwellings and never depart from their habitations.
- Strip them of their authority and cast their bands of oppression far from me.
- Thunder in the heavens and make the hearts of diviners quake and tremble.
- Utter your voice and strike them with the spirit of your tongue.
- Detain them by your power and cause their powers to become nullified in Jesus' name, amen.

Generational Curses

Scriptural Prayer Aids: Exodus 20:5-6, Deuteronomy 28:15-68, Exodus 16

- Lord, I thank you that you are a generational God.

- I pray that the plans and purposes that you have for my generations become plain in my eyes.

- Father grant me precision and accuracy concerning your blueprint for my bloodline.

- Awaken any dead or dormant possibilities you have revealed in the past.

- Let every generational sickness and disease be broken off my bloodline now in Jesus' name.

- Father, I declare that I will not be a victim of negative generational patterns.

- No family stigma will contaminate or mar my rise in Jesus' name.

- My genes which identify me with my family members will not work against me.

- I declare that no spirit of tragedy and untimely death that has raised its head in my family will stand.

- Almighty God, I ask that you cut off all unnatural and unexplainable evil that has been strategically positioned against my life.

- Let family limitations break and ordinances set to keep me stagnated receive destruction.

- By the backing authority of heaven let every ancient landmark of non-achievement give way.

- Father, I declare that negative generational patterns will not be passed down to my children.

- Almighty God reveal your blueprint for the transformation and elevate do of my bloodline.

- Give me the strategies to build solid foundations to move my family forward.

- This year I will breakthrough limitations that have held my family bound.

- Through the shed blood of the Lamb, I order a shift over my bloodline and declare that every tree not planted by God is uprooted by fire. In Jesus' name, amen.

Time Sensitive Curses

Scriptural Prayer Aids: Joshua 6:26, 1 Kings 16:34, 2 Kings 7:2

- Father, I thank you that my times and seasons are in your hands.

- I declare that time will work with me and for me and not against me.

- I ask that you restore the years that the locust, cankerworm, caterpillar, and palmerworm have eaten up out of my life.

- Let no curse set to overtake my life at a certain age materialize in Jesus' name.

- Lord, I decree that I will not become a victim of time sensitive curses present in my bloodline.

- Let every assignment of death and destruction over the men in my family be overruled and overturned.

- Nobody in my family will be cut off at an early age.

- Almighty God, let no one in my family or generations become targets because of the sins and actions of my forefathers.

- Cause all iron-like curses to be broken now in the name of Jesus.

- Let familiar spirits be dislodged and their power over my life permanently broken.

- Father blind the eyes of monitoring spirits who are tracking my life and progress.

- I command them to become immobilized and rendered powerless in Jesus' name.

- I declare that I will never be in the wrong place at the wrong time, nor in the right place at the wrong time.

- Mistaken identity for evil will not become my portion.

- Stray bullets and stray blows will never find their way into my life or the lives of my family members.

- Almighty God, let all the moments of blessing you have assigned to my life come into manifestation unhindered in Jesus' name amen.

Ancestral Wickedness

Scriptural Prayer Aids: Deut. 18 :9-13, Joshua 24 :15,

- Father in the name of Jesus let no ancestral evil coming down by bloodline become a snare in my life.
- Let every evil dedication carried out by my forefathers be overruled and reversed now.
- I nullify the activities of wasters and destroyers that have descended on my life because of wicked influences in my bloodline.
- Lord, I declare that every evil foundation must receive the judgement of God.
- Arise O God and the let idolatry is cast down and annihilated out of my family and bloodline.
- I demand the unconditional release of my loved ones from the bondage from every Jezebelic altar.
- I refuse to allow any spirit of sexual perversion to extend its reach in my bloodline.
- No consultation with witches and warlocks in the foundation of my bloodline will stand in the name of Jesus.
- I declare that the accuser of the brethren will hold nothing against my foundation.
- I refuse to become a victim of the choices and missteps of those who laid the foundation of my ancestry.
- Rewrite the story of my bloodline by your name Wonderful.
- Where there is evidence of a curse release tremendous blessings.
- Realign us and bring your blessings to bear on everything concerning us.
- Lord, I thank you for your goodness and grace in the mighty name of Jesus, amen.

Demonic Transference

Scriptural Prayer Aids: Acts 19:13-16, Luke 11:24-26, 1 Corinthians 6:16

- Father in the name of Jesus I ask that you weed out every imposter in my life.

- Let no masquerading spirit invade my life through those who I allow to enter.

- Lord, I arrest every demonic transference that has taken place in my life because of those I associate with.

- I neutralize the effects of character and destiny altering agents lurking in my environment.

- No sickness will be transferred from my friends, coworkers, patients, spouse, or family member in Jesus' name.

- Almighty God, I reject any negative pattern or cycle emanating from my workplace, industry, culture, and place of birth.

- I break the power of any negative legality I have enforced through continuous negative words I have heaped up over my own life.

- Let no unaddressed weakness cause evil spirits to be build up strongholds in my life.

- I declare that I will not attract people to me because of any weakness in Jesus' name.

- Father make it so that the mistakes of my parents, grandparents and forefathers do not attract evil spirits to me.

- Lord, I cover my ear gate and eye gate with the blood of Jesus. I declare that they will not be contaminated by anything I watch or listen to in Jesus' name.

- Remove evil deposits from my eyes and ears and soul in the name of Jesus.

- I declare that no transference will have any more progress in my life and that I will not be dominated or contaminated by them in Jesus' name, amen.

Sexual Perversion

Scriptural Prayer Aids: Leviticus 18:22, 1 Corinthians 6:18, Jude 1:7, Hosea 4: 10-19, 1 Kings 15: 9-12

- I sever every illegal soul-tie working against me in Jesus' name.

- Let no residue of past relationships or encounters remain on my life.

- Lord, I command my unconditional release from the bondage of illegal sexual encounters in Jesus' name.

- Father, I gather my emotions and declare that all emotional attachments that have sabotaged my health and wellbeing are broken.

- I collect my sexual organs from every evil altar established to prevent my marriage.

- Father let no imposter or masquerader present themselves as my spouse in Jesus' name.

- No counterfeit or spiritual assassin will have dominion over my life.

- By the shed blood of the Lamb I arrest every spirit that violates me sexually in the dream.

- I announce that your assignment is eternally revoked and that you will have no more dominion over me or my household.

- Father, I come against all forms of sexual perversion manifesting in my life.
- Through the shed blood of Jesus, I declare that all forms of sexual addiction break now.
- I confess and repent of past illicit sexual behaviour in the name of Jesus.

- Father let no spirit of sexual perversion coming down my bloodline find expression in my life.
- I come against the spirit of promiscuity and loose sexual encounters.
- Deliver me from the spirits I have taken unto myself through multiple sex partners.
- Lord let the altars raised up to sex demons through orgies, ritual sex, and the continual introduction of strangers into my matrimonial bed be destroyed.
- I arrest the stigma and trauma of rape and sexual abuse.
- Let them not cause me to develop bitterness and hatred toward the opposite sex.
- Father, I lay down every childhood sexual encounter I declare that they will not distort or inform my sexual conduct moving forward.
- Arise O God as a mighty man of war and break me free from the bondage of pornography.
- I refuse to allow images of exaggerated body parts to establish strongholds in my mind.
- Almighty God, I reject the spirit of lust and the objectifying of any person.
- Let patterns of superficial and ungodly relationships break from my life.
- I cast down the imaginations reinforced through pornography, masturbation, and sexual fetishes.
- Father let the assignment of sex demons be aborted in my life.
- I reject the spirit of fornication, adultery, and illegitimate sexual fantasies.
- I come against homosexuality, bisexuality, pansexuality, trisexuality and bestiality in the name mighty name of Jesus.
- Father, according to your lovingkindness and tender mercies let every plan of hell concerning my sexuality be disgraced.
- Today I build a defense against all forms of attack against my sexuality.

- I make the decision to live a sexually pure life and will stand my ground against all the contaminants in my environment.
- Father, I stand on your word declaring that past sexual experiences will not violate my covenant marriage.

- Lord whatever doors I have opened to allow spirit husbands/wives to thrive. I shut them now by the blood of Jesus.

- I declare my mind, emotions, will and body loosed in Jesus' name.

- Let the memory of these violations be erased forever by the blood of Jesus.

- I declare that my body is the temple of the Most High and will no longer be defiled in the name of Jesus, amen.

- By your help O God of Ebenezer, I will remain faithful in my commitment in Jesus' name, amen.

Stagnation and Stigmatization

Scriptural Prayer Aids: John 4: 5-15, 2 Kings 7:3-20, John 1:46

- Father in the name of Jesus I arrest every spirit of stagnation terrorizing my life.
- I demand unconditional release from all forms of setbacks in every area of life.
- Lord in this very hour arm me with divine speed to surpass every obstacle standing in my way.
- Anoint me to outrun the chariots on my way to destiny as you did for Elijah.
- Father let my cry trigger overnight blessings in my life in Jesus' name.
- Father, I declare that the spirit of failure will not have dominion over me.
- Almighty God, I reject the efforts of the enemy to cause me to be stuck at any stage of my life.
- Father let every spirit of castration working against my ability to produce after your order be destroyed.
- I refuse to become spiritually barren and dormant in Jesus' name.
- Let satanic limitations and restrictions break now in the mighty name of Jesus.
- Lord, I come against every assignment of shame and disgrace concerning my life.
- Father let every stigma attached to my place of birth and residence break from my life.
- Let every negativity attached to my names be revoked permanently.
- I break the power of any nickname I was given that carries a negative meaning to it.
- I reject every negative word spoken over me as a child in the name of Jesus.
- Let no negative thing transferred to me from the womb germinate in my life.
- Father, I declare that no mistake or past failure will cause to lose my good name and reputation in Jesus' name.

- Father, I thank you for your goodness and continued faithfulness towards me, in Jesus' name, amen.

Restrictions & Limitations

Scriptural Prayer Aids:

- Almighty God, by your power let all limitations and restrictions break from off my life.
- Cause everything choking out my virtue to be destroyed by the power of your might.
- Break me free of the high wall of partition between and where you have called me to be.
- Father raise me up out of the pit I am in and bring my gifts, talents and abilities into the light.
- Let every veil over my glory be permanently lifted in this season.
- For reproach O God give me favour and for obscurity grant marvelous light.
- Enlarge my territory by the power of your might and let your blessing rest heavily on me.
- Elevate me by the power of your right and never let it be lifted off me.
- Lord expose every destiny detour and sent against my rising.
- Cause every assignment assassin and destiny destroyer masquerading in my life to be exposed and rendered powerless.
- Deliver me from spirits of frustration and bitterness and help me to be promoted by your grace.
- Whoever and whatever has tried to diminish my call and anointing will be perpetually disappointed.
- Let the gates of brass and the doors of iron be destroyed for my sake.
- Almighty God, I disassociate myself from every idea that I will not progress.
- I declare that this month my mouth will be filled with extraordinary testimonies.
- Father, I thank you for increase and for divine enlargement in Jesus' name, amen.

Geographical Strongholds

Scriptural Prayer Aids: Joshua 6:1-27, 2 Chronicles 34:3-7, Mark 5:1-20

- Almighty God I ask that you move every obstacle that is planted in my environment.

- Let negative geographical strongholds begin to give way.

- By the power of your might cause territorial spirits to be bound and to be rendered powerless.

- Let their devices come to nothing and their assignment perpetually frustrated.

- Move swiftly on my behalf and let your judgement fall on every spirit blocking my progress in my community, city, and nation.

- Father strip gatekeepers of their spiritual armour and permanently remove them from their locations.

- Let locations that are prone to accidents and destruction have no dominion over me and my family.

- Let spirits that rule over the spiritual atmosphere and climate of my community not sway the minds of those positioned to bless me.

- I declare that witchcraft rituals involving the sun and moon will not strike me by day or night.

- Lord grant me divine exemption from negative climatic occurrences that dominate my location.

- I declare that I will be satisfied in famine and that at destruction and famine I will laugh.

- Almighty God, give me the keys to my city in the name of Jesus.

- Let the gates and the doors in my location begin to swing wide open for me.

- Allow me to enter in, in the spirit so I can truly enter in, in the natural.

- Let my presence open doors that have never been released in my community.

- Let this be a season of divine release and out pouring in Jesus' name.

Every Christian has been recruited as a soldier in the army of the Lord. Paul tells us that our weapons and warfare are not carnal (natural) but spiritual. We should understand that there is no way we will overcome the devil without a fight. We must be willing and ready to defend our families, homes, and communities through spiritual warfare. We also cannot hope to walk in purpose and fulfil our destinies without any demonic interference. Those who engage in spiritual warfare must also understand that it is no light thing and that it must be entered into seriously. Let us therefore, put on the whole armour of God and earnestly contend for the faith.

Seat of Authority

Scriptural Prayer Aids: Matthew 10:8, Mark 16:17, Ephesians 2: 1-6, 1 Corinthians 15:57

- Father in the name of Jesus I thank you that I am seated in heavenly places in Christ Jesus.
- Almighty God because of where I sit, I understand that I am elevated above principalities and powers.
- I declare that I will not lose ground to the enemy because of fear and timidity.
- From my seat of power, I crush every opposition under my feet.
- I refuse to fall or backslide from my position of authority.
- Let the jealously of God act swiftly on my behalf and let your enemies become as nothing.
- Father, I ask for angelic reinforcement to accomplish your exploits in the earth.

- Let my decrees be established according to your perfect will.
- I decree that every lawful and unlawful act the enemy has released against my life will be crushed under my feet.
- As the enemy raises his head he will be destroyed.
- May the one who sits upon the circle of the earth break the power of the god of this world.
- I command the communication system of the wicked one to be dismantled.
- Father let the prince of the power of the airwaves have no dominion over me.
- Today I reinforce the armour of God over my life and declare that it will remain impenetrable in Jesus' name.
- Let the shield of faith be expanded over my life, as I move from faith to faith and from glory to glory.
- When the shield is risen no fiery dart of the enemy will be left unquenched.
- I decree that no demonic conclusion in the realm of the spirit concerning my life or the lives of my family members will manifest.
- I abort every negative thing set in the womb of destiny to bring me failure and destruction.
- My headship will be continually anointed with fresh oil, and I will remain in my place of elevation.
- By the power of your might let everything in heaven and earth line up to accommodate your will in my life.
- Almighty God, grant me mastery over spiritual things so that I can triumph in all areas of my life.

- Grant me complete victory in over the works of darkness for your name's sake.
- According to your perfect will let your greatness expand over every area of my life in Jesus' name, amen.

The Womb of the Morning -*(Speaking over the first part of
the day).*
*Scriptural Prayer Aids: Exodus 16:7, Psalm 110:3, Psalm 143:8,
Lamentations 3:22-24*

Petition:
- Almighty God, I thank you that my times are in your hands.

- You are all-knowing and have already decided what must
  come to pass, in the days which are ahead of me.

- Therefore, Father, when I rise, please fill me with new
  mercies, in the name of Jesus Christ.

- I prophesy into the womb of this morning and I
  command it to hear me and respond, in the name of
  Jesus.

- I command all the hidden resources, ideas, favour and
  blessings which are laid up in this day, to be released to
  me, in the name of Jesus.

- Awaken my ears to hear what you have declared over this day.

- I declare that all the treasures of wisdom and good counsel
  that you utter in the morning will manifest in my life, in
  the name of Jesus.

- I cancel every spell and curse that the enemy, or
  witches and wizard have released over my life, today.

- I cancel every plot of untimely death and tragedy sent
  against me and my family, in the name of Jesus Christ.

- I declare that I will not be a candidate of misfortune and
  failure at any point during this day.

- Lord, cause me to see the first fruits of your glory when I
  rise in the morning.

- Cause me to capture the daily benefits you will release in
  this day, in the name of Jesus Christ.

- Cause your plans and purposes for this day to be revealed to
  me, in the name of Jesus.

- Let the insights and revelations which belong to this day become my portion.

- I declare that I will increase on every hand today, in the name of Jesus.

- I declare that all the territory I have lost, in any area of my life, will come back to me today.

- I pronounce over this day, that I will have no delays and no disappointments, when conducting my affairs.

- I declare that I will be in the right place at the right time.
- I declare that favour will find me everywhere I go today.

- Today, the works of my hands shall prosper in unprecedented ways.

- I will find prosperity and good success in this day, in the name of Jesus.

- Father, I ask for new inspiration and renewed strength to go through this day.

- Morning Star, shine upon me today and give me direction for my life.

- Glorify yourself in my life today in the name of Jesus.

- Lord, satisfy me with your unfailing love this morning, so that I may praise you all my days. Amen.

Demonic Ambushment

Scriptural Prayer Aids: Deut. 25:17-19, 1 Samuel 30, Job 1, Matthew 13:25

- Omniscient God, I thank you that all things are naked before you and that nothing takes you by surprise.

- Father let no decision be made concerning me or my family in the spiritual or natural realm without my knowledge.

- Give the enemy no executive decision-making power in any area of life or the lives of my family members.

- Father let nothing catch me off guard at any stage or in any area of my life in Jesus' name.

- Teach me to always guard and fortify my home base so that the Episode at Ziklag never plays out in my life.

- I come against the violent assault of the wicked one and declare that I will escape as a bird out of every trap set for me.

- Father, I nullify the effects of surprise attacks and demonic agendas.

- Confuse the camp the enemy and bring his communication system into total disrepair.

- Expose every spirit that seeks to camouflage itself in my environment.

- Root up evil out of its hiding places and expose the designs of hell by the light of your coming.

- I declare that I will not be ambushed when I am progressing or when I am at rest.

- Let no undetected weapon positioned against me or my family get the opportunity to be triggered or launched.

- Before they are formed O God destroy them, as they lift their heads let them be crushed.

- Lord, I thank you that you are my shield and defense in Jesus' name, amen.

Demonic Strongholds- *(demonic activity that is strong and stubborn).*

Scriptural Prayer Aids: Jeremiah 48:41, Nahum 3:12, Habakkuk 1:10

Petition:

- Father, I thank you that death and life are in the power of the tongue.

- Father as I utter these words let them come to pass speedily.

- I pronounce death upon every Goliath in my life, in the name of Jesus.

- Let every curse uttered by any proud spirit over my life be frustrated, in the name of Jesus.

- I come against every spirit of fear and intimidation, in the name of Jesus.

- I trample under foot every demon-inspired problem in my life, in the name of Jesus.

- I take up arms today in the name of Jesus and I declare that I will never be defeated.

- Defend me O God, by your mighty power, in the name of Jesus.

- Deliver my enemy into my hands in the name of Jesus.

- I pull down every negative stronghold in my life, in the name of Jesus.

- I smash every recurring problem in my life against the rock of my salvation.

- Father, remove every yoke of non-achievement in my life.

- Lord anoint me to overtake and plunder the house of the strongman, assigned against me.

- Father Lord, today, I confront and conquer every demonic stronghold in my life.

- Every stubborn and relentless problem in my life, speaking proud words against me, be brought to open shame, right now.

- Let every stubborn pursuer in my life be trampled under my feet, in the name of Jesus.

- Let every arrogant demonic spirit, speaking boastful things against me, be permanently silenced, in the name of Jesus.

- Lord empower my prayer altar in the name of Jesus.

- Let the violent assault of the enemy in my life, be brought to nothing.

- Let the hiding place of the enemy become a terror to him.

- Let the demonic strongholds operating in my family, community and nation, be displaced and scattered, in the name of Jesus.

- Let the feeding ground of the enemy in my life become desolate.

- Lord, reveal to me the things which strengthen the grip of demonic strongholds in my life.

- Lord, I will give you no rest until every demonic stronghold in my environment, is completely destroyed.

- Lord Jesus, take captivity captive in my life right now.

- Let every coffin-like spirit released against me receive the stones of fire, in the name of Jesus.

- Lord ride upon your high places as a man of war and defend my cause today.

- Deliver me out of the hand of my strong enemy who seeks to devour me.

- Let those who desire to eat me up be destroyed, in the name of Jesus.

- Let my life become too hot for the enemy to handle.

- Make my words a terror to the ears of the wicked.

- I thank you, because I know that you are the great and
  terrible God that never loses a battle. Amen.

Demonic Networks-An organization of demonic influence which resides over families, homes, communities etc.

Scriptural Prayer Aids: Nehemiah 4:8, I Samuel 13:5, Psalm 35:15, Isaiah 54:15

Petition:

- Father, I announce that the demonic forces who are gathered to do me harm shall not fulfill their cause.

- God scatter them with your world wind in the name of Jesus.

- Let the demons who have joined forces together to destroy me be bound with chains of iron.

- Cause demonic agents who conspire to do me harm be brought to utter destruction, in the name of Jesus.

- Lord let the evil spirits who conceive mischief and bring forth destruction be rendered powerless.

- Holy God, let every satanic embargo raised up against my life be utterly defeated.

- Lord of Hosts, I declare that though demonic forces may surround me like bees, they shall be cut off without remedy.

- Father, cause the strength of the wicked one to loose its hold over my life.

- Let the communication system of the demonic network assigned to my family refuse to operate.

- O God, disappoint and confound the powers of death and hell assigned against me.

- Father, expose the enemy who would disguise himself to gain advantage over me.

- Let the imposters in my environment be exposed in the name of Jesus.

- Father, let every aggression being released against my destiny be destroyed.

- Let those who are bent on cursing me be silenced in the name of Jesus.

- Lord cause the conspiracy against my success to receive your wrath.

- Let the meeting places of conspirators become dens of confusion in the name of Jesus.

- Lord fight against the demonic systems which fight against me.

- Let my prayers become like hot coals of fire in Jesus' name.

- Give me insight into the plans of the enemy before they are organized.

- Let the seed of iniquity die before it sees the sun in the name of Jesus.

- Let the reign of the wicked seize in the name of Jesus.

- Father, l command your fire to burn to consumption anything planted in my environment which is intended to spiritually paralyze.

- Father, I ask you to take up my cause with those who will help me.

- Father, though there may be many that seek after my soul you are my shield.

- Lord let the angels assigned to me intercept and destroy every demonic arrow sent against me.

- I declare that only with my eyes shall I see and behold the reward of the wicked.

- Father, let there be no regrouping and reorganization of demonic activity against my life in the name of Jesus.

- Almighty God, I declare that I will not experience any demonic counterattacks from the camp of the enemy.

- Lord show yourself strong on my behalf in this season for your name's sake, amen.

Territorial Spirits- Demonic agents who rule over specific regions (countries, parishes, states, cities) or world systems (music, fashion, economics etc).

Scriptural Prayer Aids: I Samuel 13:3, Matthew 4:16, Luke 4:14

Petition:
- Holy Father, it is written that your eyes run to and fro the earth   beholding both the evil and the good.

- Lord, I declare that the territory on which I stand belongs only to you.

- Father cause the territorial spirits who are lodged over the region where I conduct business, to be uprooted in the name of Jesus.

- Let their influence be broken from the heart and minds of those who I partner with.

- Father, I declare that every place that the sole of my foot shall tread upon is mine.

- I pronounce your rule and lordship over the country I live in.

- Protect its borders from the influence of territorial spirits in the name of Jesus.

- Father go before me against every spirit that seeks to dominate my home and family in the name of Jesus.

- Father, through your might I subdue and conquer the influence of territorial spirits in my life.

- Father, let the blood of Jesus cover everything concerning me in the name of Jesus.

- I take back every measure of spiritual territory that I have lost to the enemy through ignorance and fear.

- Lord, let the predominant sin in my bloodline break in the name of Jesus.

- Father, I cleanse my birthplace with the blood of Jesus.

- I come against anything that was in my environment as a child, which has become a snare in my life.

- I command the territorial spirits which rule over my community to scatter and to be consumed by the fire of God.

- I command the territorial spirits which rule over the poorest regions in my country, to scatter and to be consumed by the fire of God.

- I command the territorial spirits which rule over the education system in my country, to scatter and to be consumed by the fire of God.

- I command the territorial spirits which rule over the entertainment system in my country, to scatter and to be consumed by the fire of God.

- I command the territorial spirits which rule over the financial system in my country, to scatter and to be consumed by the fire of God.

- I command the territorial spirits which rule over the scientific system in my country, to scatter and be consumed by the fire of God.

- I command the territorial spirits which rule over the social system in my country, to scatter and to be consumed by the fire of God.

- I command the territorial spirits which rule over the judicial system in my country, to scatter and to be consumed by the fire of God.

- I command the territorial spirits which rule over the cultural system in my country, to scatter and to be consumed by the fire of God.

- I command the territorial spirits which rule over the nations that my country is in partnership with, to scatter and to be consumed by the fire of God.

- Father, I send warring angels before me concerning my declarations.

- Lord let none of my words fall to the ground in the name of Jesus.

Witchcraft

Scriptural Prayer Aids: 2 Chronicles 33: 1-16, Micah 5:12, Galatians 5:19-20

Petition:
- Father, I call forth the anger and rage of God against every evil altar raise up against me, in the name of Jesus.

- Let those who consult with familiar spirits to harm me be confounded and perpetually frustrated, in the name of Jesus.

- Father, overthrow every blood sacrifice which is being offered up against me, in the name of Jesus.

- Send tempest and affliction against every demonic agent who makes it their business to tamper with my life.

- Lord, release burning coals of fire against the demons that cause those they possess, to indulge in the drinking of blood and the eating of flesh, to strengthen themselves, in their wicked acts towards my home, family, community and country.

- Father, I pronounce destruction on every idol raised up in my nation which demands worship through the performance of witchcraft.

- Let those who seek the counsel of witches and warlocks be violently awaken out of their deception.

- Let every spell, incantation and curse released against me through witchcraft be rendered null and void.

- Almighty God, let those who consult with the dead to destroy me be brought to sudden and open disgrace, in the name of Jesus.

- Lord of Hosts, I command those who use plants, birds, snakes, and shells to perform their evil work to be brought to confusion.

- Holy One, I command those who use anything in the sea to perform their evil work to be brought to confusion.

- I come against superstitions and traditions in my family, community, and nation, which evoke evil spirits.

- Father let there be no doorway in my life for witchcraft to enter through.

- Lord, please paralyze the effects of every kind and form of charm erected in my environment.

- I declare that I possess the mind of Christ and I reject every mind control tactic of the enemy.

- Deliver me from every kind and form of manipulation in the name of Jesus.

- Mighty God I refuse to be manipulated by the traditions and rituals of my ancestors.

- Almighty God I refuse to be manipulated by demonic signs and wonders.

- Almighty God I refuse to be manipulated by the people around me.

- Almighty God I refuse to be manipulated by world systems.

- Almighty God I refuse to be manipulated by the philosophies of man.

- Almighty God I refuse to be manipulated by the wealth of the wicked.

- Almighty God I refuse to be manipulated by the spirits of fear and defeat.

- Almighty God I refuse to be manipulated by depression.

- Almighty God I refuse to be manipulated by carnal thinking.

- Almighty God I refuse to be manipulated by the spirit of sexual perversion.

- Almighty God I refuse to be manipulated by my relationships.

- Almighty God I refuse to be manipulated by spirits of deception.

- Almighty God I refuse to be manipulated by familiar spirits.

- Lord, I praise you for what you have done for me through this prayer. Amen.

Satanic Covenants- Any covenant or agreement entered with satan concerning your life, your family, home etc.

Scriptural Prayer Aids: Isaiah 28:18, Acts 26:18, Ephesians 3:20

Petition:
- Holy Father, I thank you that the shed blood of Jesus has brought me into an unconquerable covenant with you.

- Lord, I praise you because I know that this covenant is superior to all other covenants and that it has the power to dissolve every negative covenant that may be operating against my life.

- Father, I dissolve the effect of every satanic covenant I have entered whether consciously or subconsciously.

- I nullify the effect of any evil dedication ceremony I was initiated in as a child in the name of Jesus.

- Lord, I ask you to search my house and reveal to me any hidden object that is in it, which may have been used as a symbol of satanic covenants.

- Cause me to identify and throw out any clothes, jewelry or ornament that has been dedicated to satan.

- I come against every blood sacrifice which was undertaken by my ancestors which is now adversely affecting my life.

- I come against every covenant made with the sun, moon, and stars to make my life ineffective and unprofitable.

- I break myself loose from every demonic contract which is designed to keep me from achieving my goals.

- I nullify the effect of any covenant made to eat up my finances and keep me in poverty, in the name of Jesus.

- I nullify the effects of any covenant made on my behalf or on behalf of my family to invoke the power of spirit guides

- I refuse to be controlled by the dictates of spirit guides which have attached themselves to my life and property.

- Let the hailstones and tempest of God search out and destroy everything in my environment that has been manipulated and anointed by the occult in the name of Jesus.

- Father, let anyone in my environment and sphere of influence who has been initiated into the occult be exposed, with the light of your countenance.

- I sever every soul tie that I may have with any person, thing or place in the name of Jesus.

- Lord, I undo any damage and repair every breach that has come into my life because of sexual perversion.

- Let every door opened by rape, incest, fornication, adultery, pornography, and wrong exposure to sex, be closed forever, by the blood of the Lamb.

- Lord, I command every evil bewitchment which has presented itself in my environment, because of a satanic covenant, to be dismantled.

- Lord let the satanic covenants that have been entered into because of greed in my country, be broken in the name of Jesus.

- Let the torment of unjust financial gain lift from my community.

- Lord let the satanic covenants that have been entered into because of a lust for power, in my country, be broken in the name of Jesus.

- Almighty God, heal and deliver this nation from the influence of satanic covenants in the name of Jesus.

- Father God, glorify yourself in my life through this prayer, for your name's sake, amen.

Night Raiders- When you are assaulted in your sleep by demonic spirits. When you are attacked in your dreams and robbed of your sleep by satanic agents.

Scriptural Prayer Aids: Psalm 74:16, Psalm 91:5, Jeremiah 6:4-5, Hosea 7:1

Petition:
- Almighty God, I praise you because you rule over both day and night.

- They are your servants and must serve you and yield to your commands.

- Father, I thank you because I am assured of your faithfulness which comes to me every night.

- Lord, I ask that you deliver me from the fear of the dark in the name of Jesus.

- Father, I ask that you expose those who use the cover of night to perform evil deeds.

- Bring their plans and purposes to nought in the name of Jesus.

- Lord of Hosts, I command every demonic spy sent out against me at night to receive perpetual blindness, in the name of Jesus.

- Lord, I come against every satanic attack and assault which ambushes me in my sleep in the name of Jesus.

- I withdraw the right of any demonic spirit to visit me in the dream in the name of Jesus.

- Lord, I stand to resist the spirit of terror and panic that is released in the night season.

- I renounce any satanic covenant I have agreed to in my dreams.

- Every assignment of the waster and destroyer to attack me when I am sleeping and defenseless, receive double destruction by the hand of God.

- I plead the blood of Jesus against any sexual perversion that I may find myself engaging in, in my dreams.

- I declare that I will have nothing to do with spirit wives/husbands in the name of Jesus.

- Almighty God, I pray that my chastity will not be tampered with in my sleep in the name of Jesus.

- Father, I repent of any involvement in sexual misconduct, which has given sex demons the right to visit and torment me at nights.

- Lord, I come against any kind of mind control that visits me in the night.

- I plead the blood of Jesus against the effects of séances, cultic rituals and necromancy ceremonies which are directed against me in the night season.

- Lord of Hosts, let the demons who cause persons to fall into trances in the night, to step out of their bodies to do evil be brought to desolation.

- Let no seed of confusion be deposited in me in the night season that when I rise in the morning, I do not know how to conduct my affairs.

- Let no seed of depression be deposited in me in the night season, that when I rise in the morning I cannot function.

- Let no seed of fear be deposited in me in the night season, that when I rise in the morning, I am crippled by panic and anxiety.

- Let no seed of bitterness be deposited in me in the night season, that when I rise in the morning, I behave in an ungodly way towards others.

- Let no seed of memory loss be deposited in me in the night season, that when I rise in the morning, I cannot remember the instructions you have given.

- Let no seed of barrenness be deposited in me in the night season that when I rise in the morning, I cannot produce anything positive.

- Let no seed of backwardness be deposited in me in the night season that when I rise in the morning, the works of my hands do not prosper.

- Let no seed of deception be deposited in me in the night season that when I rise in the morning, I walk under the influence of the spirit of delusion.

- Lord, I declare that no night raider shall rob me of my virtue and blessing, in the name of Jesus, amen.

Evil Decrees
Scriptural Prayer Aids: Isaiah 10:1, Jeremiah 22:28-30, Numbers 23:23

- Father let no evil decree released against my life come into manifestation.
- Cause ordinances that attract ancient spirits attached to my bloodline lose their hold.
- I overrule everything that has been instituted into spiritual law that is designed to work against my progress and success.
- Decrees made into specific days, times and seasons for my downfall will not germinate.
- Any negative decision made by men concerning my life will come to nothing.
- Decrees for the construction of demonic strongholds in my family and bloodline be overturned now in Jesus' name.
- Let every circumstance and agency that works against your word in my life receive decrees of ruin and destruction.
- Father let these decrees manifest with great speed in Jesus' name.
- Let the woes written in scripture against those who decree unrighteous decrees be fulfilled before my eyes.
- Father let the decrees of limitation and restriction break now in Jesus' name.
- I superimpose the law of life over the law of sin and death.
- Let evil deliberations concerning my life, purpose, and future, perish in Jesus' name.
- Break the teeth of the wicked and cause their tongues to cleave to the roof of their mouths.
- Add iniquity unto the iniquity of those who assemble demonic decrees in the name of Jesus.
- I activate diplomatic immunity as an ambassador of Christ against evil decrees in Jesus' name.

- Lord, I thank you that your word will stand and will supersede the words of wicked spirits and the devil himself in the mighty name of Jesus, amen.

Satanic Altars

Scriptural Prayer Aids: Numbers 23, I Kings 18, 2 Chronicles 33:1-25, Acts 17:23

- Lord of Hosts, I cry against every evil altar militating against me in the name of Jesus.
- Let their wicked devices come to nothing and their structures come to ruin.
- Let the judgement of God fall on them without remedy and let sudden destruction become their portion.
- Cause every manifestation of these altars to be cut down and let them receive eternal fire.
- Almighty God, break the cycle of destruction being issued against me by satanic altars.
- I arrest the spirit of untimely death and tragedy in name of Jesus.
- Every altar that is strengthened by the shedding of blood receive blows from the right hand of God.
- By the superior blood of the Lamb let the blood of animals be of no effect concerning my life and destiny.
- I command those in my family that have been bound by satanic altars to be loosed now in Jesus' name.
- Father destiny dilution and manipulation that took place at any altar be permanently reversed in Jesus' name.
- Almighty God I declare that no incantation, spell, or chant uttered against at any altar will stand.
- Every altar whose assignment is to hide my glory receive eternal fire, right now in the name of Jesus.
- Altars responsible for stagnation, shame, disgrace, failure at the edge of breakthrough, hostility and heartache be destroyed without remedy.
- Arrows of destruction that are shooting at my life from satanic altars return a hundred-fold on the head of your senders in Jesus' name.

- Doors of destruction and defeat opened by satanic altars close now in the name of Jesus.
- According to your integrity O God be my rock of deliverance and strong tower in Jesus' name, amen.

Tragedy & Untimely Death
Scriptural Prayer Aids:

- Father in the name of Jesus deliver me from all forms of evil in Jesus' name.
- I rebuke, cast down and dismantle the operation of tragedy against every area of my life.
- I declare that me nor my family members will become victims of tragedy.
- Lord by the power of your might destroy the power of those conspiring against my safety.
- Cast down every evil imagination against my life, family and calling.
- I will not be in the wrong place at the wrong time, nor will I become a victim of stray bullets and stray blows.
- I come against vehicle accidents and freak accidents.
- My life will not be cut short because of my environment or my bloodline.
- I disassociate myself from every kind and form of activity that will shorten my days.
- I profess that as I child of God I will be far from trouble and that my days will be spent in rest.
- Father, even when a thousand fall at my side and ten thousand at by right side I will not be harmed.
- I declare divine immunity from all forms of sickness and disease, viruses and any biological weapon that may manifest on the earth.
- I declare that with long life you will satisfy me and show me your salvation.
- I will produce fruit at an old age and will fulfill the full measure of my days.
- My assignment will be completed, and I will have time to enjoy the fruits of my labour in Jesus' name, amen.

Demonic Delays
Scriptural Prayer Aids: Daniel 12-17, Ezekiel 12:21-28, Deuteronomy 7:10, Romans 13:11

- Father in the name of Jesus let divine speed overtake every area of my life.
- Let the destruction that walks with delay pass over me and my household in Jesus' name.
- Let demonic gatekeepers fall and die and let their habitations become perpetually desolate.
- Father, I declare that my angels of blessing will not be detained by demonic forces.
- Almighty God, I refuse to allow hope that is deferred to cause me to become emotionally and physically ill.
- Father let this be the set time that you will rise and favour me in Jesus' name.
- Lord make haste to help and to deliver me so that negative situations are not prolonged in my life.
- Satisfy me early with your goodness so that men may know that there is a God in Israel.
- Father do a new thing in my life and cause it to spring up now in Jesus' name.
- I declare that I will not suffer loss due to undue delay.
- I command all forms of detention in my life to crumble and fall.
- I refuse to remain in a state of stagnation; ever rehearsing and never getting on the stage of life.
- Let the chains of stagnation and detention break from off my life and let the violent assault of the enemy on my progress come to an end.
- Father give the enemy no room to frustrate the answers to my prayers, and by the power of your might bring them into full manifestation.
- Lord, I thank you that you are the God of speed and that you will move swiftly on my behalf in Jesus' name, amen.

Satanic Agents

*Scriptural Prayer Aids: John 8:44, II Corinthians 11:15,
1 John 4:1*

- Great and terrible God unmask every imposter and masquerader in my life.
- Let no witch or warlock walking around in my environment contaminate my spiritual atmosphere.
- I take authority over any agency of hell manifesting against my life.
- Let those that have been assigned against my life using religion be rendered powerless.
- Lord grant me discernment in my walk with you and teach me how to try the spirits.
- Deliver me from the spirit of the Anti-Christ in whatever shape or form it presents itself.
- Lord, I declare that I will not be led astray by false teachers and false signs.
- Father whoever is planted in my life that you have not ordained let them be uprooted now in Jesus' name.
- Almighty let no destiny killer and spiritual abortionist worm their way into my life.
- Almighty God, let satanic agents planted in my place of work and in my industry receive divine judgement.
- Let no conspiracy against my life, ministry and progress be hindered by satanic agents.
- Cause the enemy's lust against my life to be turned into shame and disgrace.
- Father any sleep undertaken to perform astral projections against my life become dead sleep.
- Deliver me from any kind and form of evil manifesting in my environment because of satanic agents.
- Shield and defense raise up a standard of help and victory for me in Jesus' name, amen.

PART VI

PRAYER FOR THE CHURCH

The Church is the Bride of Christ. His precious blood was shed for her and He is jealous over His heritage. The God of this world and its systems, hates the Church and is bent on destroying her at any cost. We must pray for each other so that we may all be able to stand in these last days.

Unity

Scriptural Prayer Aids: Genesis 11:6, Psalm 133:1, John 17:20-2.

Petition:

- Almighty God, I come to you once more, in the name of Jesus.

- Father, I realize that the body of Christ can accomplish very little when it is divided.

- So I ask you, to break down the walls of partition among us, in the name of Jesus.

- I repent, of everything that I have done, to cause division in Jesus' name.

- Father, deliver us from prejudice and pride, in the name of Jesus.

- Let there be no room in us to harbour unforgiveness, maliciousness and offence.

- Father, purge us from every kind and form of slander, rebellion and disobedience, in the name of Jesus.

- Cause every spirit of disorder, confusion and turmoil to cease from among us, in the name of Jesus.

- I close the door to every evil work that may be operating in the Church because of disunity.

- Father, cause us to walk in unity, so we may be preserved from the evil of the times.

- Lord, make us one so that the world may believe in you.

- Give us one heart and one purpose in matters concerning your kingdom.

- Let rivalry and competition be no more mentioned among us, in the name of Jesus.

- Help us to submit to each other so that the work of the Lord will not be hindered.

- Father, we long for your glory, make us one so that your glory can truly shine down on us.

- Lord, visit our churches and remove everything that causes contention and strife.

- Holy Father, heal our churches of conflict and power struggles, in the name of Jesus.

- Purify our motives and purge our hearts almighty God.

- Help us to understand that we are all connected and all need each other.

- Help us to see that each of our individual visions is a part of your holistic vision.

- Make us aware of the fact that the body of Christ was never intended to be divided.

- Help us to understand that a kingdom that is divided against itself cannot stand.

- Let the unity of the Church start with me in the name of Jesus.

- Teach me how to walk in humility and help me to submit myself to those who have been called to lead.

- Let me not be party to slander and backbiting in the name of Jesus.

- Father, help me not to participate in anything that will strengthen the divide in the body of Christ.

- Father, set a guard over my tongue so that it is not used to tear down the body of Christ.

- Rather, let my words become like medicine to those who have been offended by the Church, in one way or the other.

- Father, make me a repairer of the breach and an agent of change.

- Holy One, I honour you for granting this request, in Jesus' name. Amen.

Revival

Scriptural Prayer Aids: Psalm 138:7, Isaiah 57:15, Hosea 14:7, Habakkuk 3:2

Petition:

- Father, I thank you that all gifts and callings come from you.

- Father of Light, reveal every gift and talent you have deposited in the Church for this season.

- Give us the wisdom to use them and to bring them into maturity.

- Lord, cause the body of Christ to stir up every gift you have given it, in the name of Jesus.

- Cause the Church to take hold of the blessing and prosperity, which come with using its gifts.

- Lord, I paralyse every destiny killer that wars against the body of Christ, in the name of Jesus.

- Purge us as believers of inconsistency and time wasting, in the name of the Lord Jesus.

- Give us the discipline to do what is required, for the glory of the Church to be fully expressed.

- Anoint us with the spirit of excellence in the name of Jesus.

- Father, cause the body of believers to boldly express their gifts, just the way you intended them to.

- I prophesy over every dead gift, talent and ability in the churches and I command them to come alive.

- I declare that every believer shall become all that you called them to become, from the foundations of the world.

- I decree that we shall become great and our name shall be made great.

- I declare that no weakness or habitual sin will keep the believers from reaching their full potential in you.

- Lord, let every self-destructive tendency in the body of Christ die, in the name of Jesus.

- Holy God, revive us and we will call upon your name.

- Mighty God, resurrect purpose and destiny in our lives.

- Remove the scales of religious mechanics from our eyes.

- Fall upon us like a flood O Lord, in the mighty name of Jesus.

- We seek you and no one else can grant us the desires of our hearts.

- Father, some of us have been spoilt and ravished by the enemy but we call on your great name today.

- Heal our backslidings and cause us to return to you completely.

- Increase us on every hand and enlarge our borders, in the name of Jesus.

- Father Lord, empower every believer to maximize the anointing on their lives.

- Let the greater works of the spirit be manifested through your Church, in the name of Jesus.

- Lord, I thank you that you will accomplish your desire in us, in Jesus' name. Amen.

Reform

Scriptural Prayer Aids: 1 Chronicles 12:32, Psalm 11:3, Zecheriah 2:2, Hebrews 9:8-10

Petition:

- Almighty God, let your order prevail in the body of Christ.

- Deliver us of every kind and form of confusion and disorder, in the name of Jesus.

- Father, please visit the foundation of the various churches and remedy any structural weakness therein.

- Resurrect your truth wherever it has fallen in the Church.

- Cause those who lead to come to the full understanding of their offices and ranks.

- Father, lovingly, reveal anything in our belief system that is contrary to your word.

- Deliver the Church from the spirit of error in the name of Jesus.

- Grant unto our leaders vision and revelation, far beyond the scope of what they have already experienced.

- Lord, usher us into a new era of power and purpose, in the name of Jesus.

- Make me a part of the change that you desire to bring to the body of Christ.

- Help me to play my part in repairing the spiritual desolation, of this generation.

- Fill the Church with the spirit of the pioneer that we may accomplish the impossible.

- Raise up among us reformers and revivers in the name of Jesus.

- Father, cause the Church to break into new ground in the spirit and to take territory.

- Let the anointing of the sons of Issachar fall mightily upon us.

- Cause us to understand the times and know what is needed for the hour that we live in.

- Cause us to know you in the freshness of your anointing.

- Bring us on the cutting edge of what you are doing in your kingdom.

- Deliver us from stagnation and the traditions of men, in the name of the Lord Jesus.

- Lord give us the ability to embrace progressive revelation for every area of the Church.

- Take us into territory that humanity has never touched, in the name of the Lord Jesus.

- Compass us about with creative ideas and cause us to tap into new inventions for your glory.

- Father, cause every believer to become a bold trend setter, in the place you have called them to serve.

- Let new dimensions of your will and purpose be fulfilled in our lives.

- Cause us to rise out of mediocrity and take our rightful place in your kingdom.

- Father, pour out on us the spirit of grace and supplication like never before.

- Let your house truly be called the house of prayer in this season.

- O Lord, let your will be done in your Church as it is already done in heaven.

- Lord, position us to achieve what no other
  generation of believers has achieved, in the name
  of Jesus. Amen.

Spiritual Protection

*Scriptural Prayer Aids: Psalm 24:8, Psalm 34:7, Psalm 46:1,
   Isaiah 59:19*

   Petition:

- Almighty God, let the blood of Jesus cover everything concerning the Church, in the name of Jesus.

- Let the wall of fire be constantly around our lives, in the name of Jesus.

- I place a blood mark around the family of every believer and I declare that the enemy will not cross over.

- Father, cause the Church to aggressively take back every measure of spiritual territory, which has been lost to the enemy.

- I place the blood mark over the borders of the Church and I pray that its borders will not be penetrated by evil forces.

- Father, become the watchman on the wall of the Church, in the name of Jesus.

- Preserve us from all evil by the power of the blood of Jesus.

- Father, it is written that one shall chase a thousand and two shall put ten thousand to flight, fulfill this scripture mightily through the Church.

- Lord, cover the Church from the pestilence which walks in darkness and from the terror that lurks about at night.

- God, build up a wall of defence over our homes and let no plague come near us.

- Even if a thousand fall at our side and ten thousand at our right hand, make it so that no evil befall us.

- Holy God, I declare that the destruction that wastes at noonday will not overcome any believer.

- Lord of Hosts, send the fear and the dread of God before your people, in the name of Jesus.

- Cause your name to become a strong tower to us and let us continually resort to it.

- Lord God, please preserve us from the evil in the world, in the name of Jesus.

- Help us to understand that there are more with us, than those who are against us.

- Open our eyes to see the angelic host which is at our disposal.

- Lord, send forth warring angels to defend us against the ambushment of the devil.

- God of Jacob defend the cause of the Church in the name of Jesus.

- Be among us as a mighty man of war and do battle on our behalf.

- The God to whom vengeance belongs, arise in your fury and avenge us of our adversary the devil.

- Father keep us alert and watchful in the name of Jesus.

- Help us to be always fully covered with the armour of the Lord.

- Keep us from those who desire to devour us, in the name of Jesus.

- Lord, I thank you that when the righteous cry you will hear and deliver.

- Save us from our strong enemies in the name of Jesus.

- In the day of trouble hear us speedily and grant us swift deliverance.

- Father, because we trust in you, make us as mount Zion which cannot be moved.

- Lord, I am confident because you are in our midst and therefore we cannot be overthrown.

- Almighty God, I celebrate you because you are valiant in battle and you who will crush the head of those who rise up against us. Amen.

Signs & Wonders

Scriptural Prayer Aids: Daniel 6:27, Mark 16:17, Acts 2:43

Petition:

- Father, we have received the promised Holy Spirit, through your Son Jesus Christ.

- Through your Spirit we have access into the supernatural realm where you rule.

- So I ask that the supernatural power of your presence invade our natural existence.

- Let the Spirit of Elijah, manifest mightily in this generation, in the name of Jesus.

- Cause the miraculous to become a part of our daily experience.

- According to our faith let it be unto us, in the name of Jesus.

- Cause our shadows to become instruments of healing and deliverance.

- Cause the enemy to be rebuked by our very presence, in the name of Jesus.

- Become a great and terrible God in the midst of your people.

- Father, I ask that you give us authority over the air, land and sea.

- Father, let the knowledge of your glory cover the earth through our lives.

- Father let unusual miracles be wrought through our hands.

- Grant us great measures of revelation and insight, into the principles which govern your kingdom.

- Let the miraculous become second nature to us.

- Father, grant us the grace to make the raising of the dead a consistent occurrence.

- Holy One of Israel, cause us to take off all the limits and boundaries we have placed on you.

- Take us into the overflow of your presence and power.

- Freely move among your people Almighty God.

- I declare that we will heal the sick and cast out devils, in the name of Jesus.

- Father remove every stumbling block in our lives.

- Let a hunger for the supernatural envelope your Church once more.

- Let urgent, desperate, prayers be sent from the heart of every believer who desires to walk in the supernatural.

- Father help us not to settle or accept anything less, than what you have provided for us.

- Help us to understand that a Christian life without signs and wonders is dysfunctional.

- O God, cause us to tarry no longer in the shallow, safe places in the spirit realm, but to plunge into the deep.

- Bread of heaven, feed us until we are full of the knowledge of the limitless and amazing power of our maker.

- Holy Father, empower us so we may believe the impossible.

- Let faith become our substance and let it be evidence of the things we hope for.

- Cause us to access the invisible realm and release the things, which have yet to manifest on the earth.

- Ancient of Days, I thank you for perfecting your will in the Church in Jesus' name. Amen.

Kingdom Dominion

Scriptural Prayer Aids: Genesis 1:26, Joshua 18:1, Luke 10:19, Romans 8:37

Petition:

- Father, I thank you that you have made us kings and priests according to your perfect will.

- Lord, I declare you king over my life, in the name of the Lord Jesus.

- Your kingdom come and your will be done in the life of the Church, in the name of the Lord Jesus.

- Lord, let every other kingdom that may be reigning in it fall in the name of Jesus Christ.

- Almighty God, teach us how to rule and reign as kings on the earth.

- This day, I decree that the Church will walk in the dominion you have given it.

- I take authority over every limitation, weakness or demonic activity that may be operating against the body of Christ.

- Lord, I thank you that because we are believers, we are seated in heavenly places with Christ Jesus.

- Because of the work that was done on Calvary, the Church has been given power over all of the power of the enemy.

- The authority that Adam lost has now been given to the Church and the rights that were taken from him are now restored to every believer.

- Father, position the Church so that we will walk in all the authority, which Adam walked in before the fall.

- Let the gospel of the kingdom-reign and rule of Christ, be ever on our lips.

- Awaken our consciousness to understand, that it is indeed time for us to rule and reign on the earth.

- Father teach us how to dominate and subdue the earth.

- Lord Jesus, by your power and glory subdue and conquer all the kingdoms of the world.

- Ancient of Days, sit as king over all the nations of the earth, in the name of Jesus.

- Let the governmental authority of the kingdom of God, manifest through the Church.

- Father, I decree that the kingdom rule of God will manifest everywhere I go.

- Let the believers truly know what it means to be ambassadors of heaven.

- Raise up Christians who will bring the counsel of heaven to earth.

- Those of us who live in the heavenly realm and are dwellers on earth, shall rule from both dimensions, in the name of Jesus.

- Cause the darkness of this world to submit to the dictates of the Church.

- Raise up believers who will defy and exercise immunity over the laws of time, space and nature.

- Come kingdom of God. Come and rule, dominate and subdue the earth.

- Let the nations stand still and know that you alone are God.

- Lord, position the Church to become the means through which you are exalted in all the earth.

- Let those who put their trust in you go forth conquering, in every area of life.

- To you be glory, dominion and power now and evermore. Amen.

<u>*PART VII*</u>
<u>*PRAYER FOR COMMUNITIES*</u>

When God divided the children of Israel into tribes, he awakened in them the spirit of community. Jesus encouraged us to love our neighbours as ourselves. A part of that love should manifest itself through prayerful concern. We should feel the burden of the Lord's heart for our communities and dedicate ourselves whole-heartedly to prayer, until we see transformation manifest in them.

Protection

Scriptural Prayer Aids: *Deuteronomy 8:7, Nehemiah 9:24-25, Zechariah 8:4*

Petition:

- Lord, I thank you for always being a fence around this community.

- Father, cause this community to tap into the boldness of your presence and power.

- I come against the spirit of torment and dread that is resident in this community.

- I pronounce double destruction upon every devouring spirit in this community.

- Let the tactics of sudden death, which seeks to ambush this community at noonday, be destroyed, in the name of Jesus.

- Father, teach the hands of the occupants of this community to war and their fingers to fight, as they engage the enemy concerning this community.

- Father, I declare that no calamity or plague will visit this community, in the name of Jesus.

- Lord, expose the evil schemes of the enemy and strip the evil powers over this community, of their authority.

- Make this community inaccessible to the wicked, in the name of Jesus.

- Cause those who encamp against this community, to utterly fall, in the name of Jesus.

- Father, let the blood of Jesus cover this community.

- I plead the blood of Jesus against every attack and assault of the wicked one, in the name of Jesus.

- I place the bloodline around this community, in the name of Jesus.

- I lift up the blood of Jesus against the territorial spirit assigned to this community, in the name of Jesus.

- I plead the blood of Jesus against the demonic network in this community and I command it to be permanently destroyed.

- I plead the blood of Jesus over the minds of the people in this community, who are trapped in the deception of the enemy.

- I plead the blood of Jesus in the four corners of this territory, in the name of Jesus.

- Father, through the blood of Jesus scatter, confuse, torment, blind and paralyse, the evil powers which have set themselves up in this area.

- Let the blood of Jesus become a fierce weapon against the workers of iniquity in this community.

- Let the blood of Jesus prevail against all forms and kinds of wickedness, which manifests in this community.

- Father, as these prayer points penetrate the atmosphere, hasten the performance of your will through them. Amen.

Proclamation of Blessing

Scriptural Prayer Aids: Deuteronomy 15:4, Isaiah 61:7, Zechariah 2:12

Petition:

- Lord cause the words that I utter over this place, to become lively and active.

- I speak life over every area of this community, in the name of Jesus.

- I prophesy into the tomorrow of this community and I declare that the days which are to come, will be the best days that this community has ever seen.

- I speak into the heavens today and I command the resources which are laid up there, to be released over this community.

- I release the blessings of the Lord over every family in this place, in the name of Jesus.

- Lord, I ask that you cancel the effect of any negative word that has been spoken over this community.

- Cause the things you have declared over this community, from the foundations of the world, to manifest mightily.

- Create new expressions of your glory in this community through the power of the spoken word.

- I subdue and conquer every form of spiritual pollution in this place.

- Let transformation come to this community in the name of Jesus.

- Lord make this community a praise in the earth.

- Make its name great and establish its doings.

- Father, cause the impossible to manifest itself in this place.

- Though the enemy may have come into this community one way, I declare that he will flee several ways.

- Almighty God, cause your order to step into this place and remove every kind of confusion.

- Lord, let your peace which passes all understanding rest upon this community.

- Preserve the strength and honour of this community, in the name of Jesus.

- Lord make this place a delight to live in and a pleasant place to bring up children.

- Let your praise be constantly heard in the streets and cause your glory to shine from the faces, of those who dwell in it.

- I believe, therefore I have spoken, let my words come to pass for your name's sake. Amen.

Destiny Fulfillment

Scriptural Prayer Aids: Ecclesiastics 10:17, Isaiah 14:24, Jeremiah 29:11

Petition:

- Lord, I thank you that you are the only one who can decide the future of (name the community).

- Almighty God, bring this community into alignment with your will.

- Lord, cause the purpose and destiny of this community to be fulfilled, in the name of Jesus.

- Let everything in this community which actively resists your will; begin to give way, now.

- Make this community a place of blessing in this country, in the name of Jesus.

- Make it a model for other communities to follow.

- Make it an agent of change in this society, in the name of Jesus.

- Cause good things to come from this community for your name's sake.

- Let those speaking evil about it see it in its finest hour.

- Let this be the day that visionary leadership emerges in this community.

- Father, cause the Christians in this community to continuously pray for its welfare.

- Father, let the geographical location of this community work in its favour.

- Lord, let your holy angels take up residence in this community.

- Let every negative word spoken to overthrow the purpose of this community, be nullified.

- Father, cement your will in the hearts and minds of the citizens of (name community).

- Strengthen them as they keep the vision of (name community) alive.

- Lord, I ask that you do not take your hand off this community, until it accomplishes its destiny. Amen.

PART VIII
PRAYER FOR THE NATION

Ancestral Corruption

Scriptural Prayer Aids: Deuteronomy, 19:9-10, Leviticus 26:45

Petition:

- Lord, I thank you that you created (mention the nation) for a divine purpose.

- Father, revisit this nation in its youth and uproot every illegal transaction which occurred in it.

- Let every evil plantation be purged out of its foundation, in the name of Jesus.

- Let every act of wickedness and injustice, which marred this nation's character, be washed away forever, by the blood of Jesus.

- Let every altar raised up to idols in the formation of this nation, which continue to influence it today, be smashed to pieces, on the rock of my salvation.

- Let every blood covenant made with familiar spirits, spirit guides, witches and warlocks, be nullified by the blood of Jesus.

- Lord, I ask that you remove the curses associated with the shedding of innocent blood, at any period, in the history of this nation.

- Let every evil pronouncement spoken over this nation, through incantations, spells and negative words, loose their hold right now.

- Father, I renounce this nation's indulgence, in any form of sexual perversion, at any point in its history, in the name of Jesus.

- Almighty God, I renounce this nation's involvement, in the occult at any time in its history.

- Lord, I renounce the effects of child sacrifice, which may have taken place at any point, in this nation's history, in the name of Jesus.

- Father, let any portion or portions of the land in this nation, which may have been dedicated to idols or evil spirits, be purged by the blood of the Lamb.

- Lord, let any transaction which has taken place in this nation, that sold it into bondage, be nullified, in the name of Jesus.

- Let the effects of every form of robbery and trickery, dealt out to anyone at anytime, in this nation, be reversed.

- Let every form of political corruption and perversion, which has polluted this nation be cast out of it permanently.

- Lord, cause every effect of the illegal overthrow of government, which has released spirits of anarchy and rebellion, break, in the name of Jesus.

- Let every evil altar raised up in this nation, which demands the blood of its citizens, be completely destroyed by the Lion of Judah.

- Let all consultations with the sun, moon and stars, concerning the destiny of this nation, be nullified, in the name of Jesus.

- Father, I ask that you break every ancestral curse from off of this nation.

- Lord, let the strongman of ancestral yokes be displaced and bound, in the name of Jesus.

- Lord, let all consultations made with the dead, concerning the destiny of this nation, be neutralized, in the name of Jesus.

- Father, let all aspects of this nation's culture, which invokes ancestral spirits, be cleansed by the blood of the Lamb.

- Let the rituals and ceremonies under taken in this nation, which involve the consumption of food offered to idols, be rendered powerless, in the name of Jesus.

- I renounce the dedication of this nation to satan, in any kind or form, in the name of Jesus.

- Lord, bring this nation into divine order, in the name of Jesus.

- Position this nation to become a force to be reckoned with in the earth.

- Father, I thank you for renewing the hope of this nation in Jesus' name. Amen.

Godly Dedication

Scriptural Prayer Aids: Prov. 14: 34, Isaiah 62:6, Malachi 3:12

Petition:

- Father, I dedicate this nation to you in the name of Jesus.

- I pray that your glory will rest on it.

- Cause every spiritual blessing that you have for this nation, to be released upon it.

- Father, I dedicate the natural resources of this nation to you, in the name of Jesus.

- Father, I repent on the behalf of this country, for the abuse and mismanagement of its natural resources.

- Lord, I ask that you preserve (name the nation)'s natural resources in the name of Jesus.

- I dedicate the wealth of this nation to you in the name of Jesus.

- Lord, I lay the finance of this nation before you and I ask that you purify it.

- As (name the nation) honours you with its substance cause it to prosper.

- Revive this economy and cause the financial doors that have been shut in the past, to swing wide open, in the name of Jesus.

- Cause wealth yielding ideas to be released in this nation beyond measure.

- Send us righteous investors in Jesus' name.

- Lord I dedicate the people of this nation to you.

- I ask that you work out the purpose of this nation through each of them.

- God, from this moment let nothing that would defile what has been dedicated to you, prevail, in the name of Jesus.

- I declare that you are the God of this nation and no other god shall rule over it. Amen.

Government

Scriptural Prayer Aids: Judges 5:9, Prov. 21:1, Jeremiah 23:5, I Timothy 2:1-4

Petition:

- Almighty God, I thank you that all power in heaven, on earth and underneath the earth, is in your hand.

- You are the one who sets up rulers Father God.

- You raise up one and bring down another, all in your time.

- Father, I place the leadership of (name the nation) before you in the name of Jesus.

- From before the foundation of the world was laid, you ordained and determined the characteristics, of the leadership of this country.

- Father, it is written that the heart of the king is in your hand and you will turn it however you choose to.

- Therefore Lord, I ask that you turn the heart of the chief leader in this nation towards you.

- Grant him/her counsel from on high in the name of Jesus.

- Father, let no leader in this country use their influence to manipulate and oppress, those they have been called to serve.

- Purify the motives of those who lead this country, in the name of Jesus.

- Give them a heart for the people, Almighty God.

- Father, I repent on their behalf and ask that you cause them to submit to the power of your right hand.

- Let those political leaders, who are involved in criminal activity, be dealt with as you see fit.

- Deal with those whose only concern is to rob and plunder the nation, they have been called to serve, as you see it.

- Lord God, I renounce the involvement that any political leader may have in the occult, in the name of Jesus.

- Let our political leaders not be deceived and overtaken by the devil.

- Father God, help them to conduct themselves in godly reverential fear, in the name of Jesus.

- I renounce the involvement that any political leader may have, in the practice of sexual perversion.

- Lord, I renounce the involvement that any political leader may have, in the formation of criminal organizations.

- Holy One, I renounce the involvement that any political leader may have, in the perversion of justice.

- God of my fathers, heal and deliver our political leaders, from all forms and kinds of bondage in the name of Jesus.

- Deliver them out of the kingdom of darkness and cause them to enter into the kingdom of light.

- Save them O God by the power of your might.

- Father, cause them to make godly decisions that will further your righteous cause, in the name of Jesus.

- Lord, I renounce any demonic influence over the passing of laws in this country, in the name of Jesus

- Mighty God, I ask that you intervene in the making of the laws of this nation.

- Let the strongman, who has set himself up over the government in this country, be permanently bound, in the name of Jesus.

- I declare that righteousness will exalt this nation.

- Father let your justice prevail in this country, in the name of Jesus.

- Give (name the head of the nation) divine wisdom in conducting the affairs of (name the nation).

- Steer him/her along the right path at all times, so that the nation may be led to its destiny.

- Thank you Lord for influencing the leadership of this nation. Amen.

Peace & Protection

Scriptural Prayer Aids: Ex. 33:13, Deuteronomy 26:15, Psalm 122:6-7

Petition:

- Father Lord, I pray for the peace of (mention the nation) in the name of Jesus.

- I come against every plan of the enemy to fill this nation with terror, in the name of Jesus.

- Cover the armed forces O God and give them direction in their service to the nation.

- I pray that they will not use their power as an occasion to oppress the citizens of this country.

- Lord, let none of those who have been appointed to uphold the law be party to any illegal activity.

- Help them to carry out their duties in the fear of the Lord.

- Let every spirit of bloodshed and murder, be permanently cast out of this nation, in the name of Jesus.

- Place an impenetrable shield of your presence and power over this country.

- Keep us safe from panic, dread and despair, in the name of Jesus.

- Lord of Hosts, defend us from the onslaught of the enemy, in the name of Jesus.

- Let your peace which passes all understanding penetrate the atmosphere of this country.

- Father, let the criminal network/s in this country be confused and be permanently scattered, in the name of Jesus.

- Let the territorial princes which rule over the crime ravished communities in this nation, be permanently displaced.

- Send tempest, hail and fire, upon the evil spirits which have joined forces against this nation.
- Let their cords of unity to be broken and make it impossible for them to regroup or reinforce themselves, against this nation.

- Father, cause those who desire to enslave the youth in this nation, in a life of crime and violence, be continually disappointed.

- O God, snatch the young ones of (name the nation) as branches from the consuming fire of (name the criminal activity/ies) in Jesus' name.

- What the enemy has meant for evil in (name the nation) I pray that you will turn it around for good.

- Keep our children safe from rape, incest, molestation and brutality in the name of Jesus.

- Make the streets of (name the name) safe for them to walk and play in, in the name of Jesus.

- Cause this nation to be ranked among the safest places on earth.

- Cause the citizens of the nation to sleep in God given peace, in the name of Jesus.

- Let your angelic host guard the points of entry and exist in this country.

- Raise up intercessors who will constantly pray for its welfare.

- Make (name the nation) a haven for people and a sought after destination.

- Father, I glorify your name for bringing the words of this prayer to pass, in the name of Jesus. Amen.

Salvation

Scriptural Prayer Aids: 1 Chronicles 16:35-36, 2 Chronicles 7:14

Petition:

- God of my salvation, hear me in the name of Jesus.

- It is not your will that any should perish but that all men should be saved.

- Father, open the eyes of the Church to see the harvest you have called it to reap in this country.

- Save this nation from self-destruction, in the name of Jesus.

- Cause the message of the gospel to reach to the core of this nation.

- Remove the scales of spiritual blindness, from the eyes of the people, so that they can truly see their state.

- Save the young men almighty God and let them flee from the vanity in the world.

- Lord, awaken God consciousness in this nation like never before.

- Cause men and women to see the destructiveness of a sinful lifestyle.

- Let conviction run in the streets of (name the nation) like great showers of rain.

- Pull those who are yours out of the bed of fornication, rum bars, gambling dens and drug huts, in the name of Jesus.

- Cause those who are drunk with the seduction of this world to become drunken with your Spirit.

- Let men acknowledge the true and living God in this nation, like never before.

- Cause those who are lifted up in pride and arrogance to bow before you, almighty God.

- Let the heart of the stubborn and resistant surrender wholeheartedly before you.

- Thank you for turning this nation towards you Father in Jesus' name. Amen.

The Bible says that it is a good thing to give thanks unto the Lord (Ps. 92:1). Sometimes when we are faced with challenging circumstances we tend to forget the goodness of God. No one likes it when their efforts are unappreciated and when those around them are constantly complaining. In the same breath, when we complain we grieve the Holy Spirit. I pray that from now on, we will make the effort to see the goodness of the Lord in the land of the living. These prayer points will cause God to inhabit your praise and will cause him to work swiftly on your behalf.

Life & Health

Scriptural Prayer Aids: Psalm 3:5, Psalm 21:3-5, Jer. 30:17, 3 John vs 2

Petition:

- My Father, this is the day that you have made and I will be glad and I will rejoice in it.

- Lord, I thank you for sparing my life to see a new day.

- I laid down and slept and I woke up because you preserved me.

- I thank you that I am in my right mind and that the perils of this age have not been allowed to overwhelm me.

- I thank you for preventing me from having a nervous breakdown.

- I thank you that you have kept me from the attacks of murderers, in the name of Jesus.

- Thank you Father that my life is covered under divine purpose.

- Father, I give you praise because I have the use of my hands and feet.

- I thank you that I am not sick unto death.

- I thank you for keeping my body, from the toxic elements in my environment.

- Lord, I praise you because my bodily functions are still in tack.

- Father, I thank you because with long life you shall satisfy me and show me your salvation.

- Almighty God, I thank you that I am fearfully and wonderfully made.

- I thank you that you are my Balm in Gilead.

- I am grateful that the Son of Righteousness with healing in his wings, will rise up on my behalf.

- Lord, I thank you that because of the shed blood of Jesus Christ, I will be made whole from every sickness and disease in my body.

- Thank you Father that I am not in and out of the hospital.

- Lord, I praise you that I can breathe without difficulty.

- Thank you for preserving my sight and my hearing, in the name of Jesus.

- Thank you for the ability to speak and think without difficulty.

- Holy Father, you are awesome and always worthy to be praised in Jesus' name, Amen.

Provision

Scriptural Prayer Aids: Job 5:22, Psalm 37:25, Matthew 6:33

Petition:

- Lord, I am grateful that you have provided me with a job.
- I repent, of constantly complaining about the conditions that I have to work under.
- Help me to realize that I have this job for a specific purpose, which I must fulfill before I can move on.

- Thank you for food and even though I may not have enough all the time, I am grateful that I am not at the point of starvation.
- Lord, I thank you for shelter and a place to rest my head.
- Father, thank you for supplying my financial needs.
- Lord, you have been faithful to me and I am grateful.
- Father, I thank you for the provision of the blood of Jesus Christ.
- Through His blood I have access to your throne.
- Lord, thank you that I can be cleansed by the blood of the Lamb, from all my sins.
- Thank you for showing up on my behalf whenever I am in need.
- Lord, I appreciate the sunshine, the moonlight, the birds and the trees.
- Father, thank you that I have free access to water.
- Lord, thank you for clothes and shoes.\
- Thank you that I have freedom to worship you in the open.
- Thank you that I have free access to an education.

- Lord I am grateful that I can call on you at any time and in any place.
- Thank you that I have access to hearing and reading your word.

- Father, I will rejoice before you because you take care of all my needs.

- I praise, honour and give you thanks in the name of Jesus. Amen.

Protection

Scriptural Prayer Aids: Psalm 37:11, Isaiah 57:2, Luke 1:79, Romans 5:1

Petition:

- Lord, I thank you that no evil has come near my dwelling.

- I thank you that those who would have come upon me, to eat up my flesh, have stumbled and have fallen.

- Father, I thank you that when I looked for the oppressor, he was nowhere to be found.

- I thank you because your name has become a strong tower for me on my many occasions.

- Lord thank you that the battles that I face do not belong to me but to you.

- Father, I praise you because you promised that you would fight for me.

- Lord, I give you glory because you have taught me how to indulge in intelligent warfare.

- Holy One, I am grateful that none of the arrows of the enemy have wounded me.

- Lord, I thank you that you have caused me to escape, out of the hand of the enemy.

- Thank you for preserving me from the assault, of the enemy.

- Lord, thank you for keeping my loved ones from calamity.

- Thank you for being a shield for me in the name of Jesus.

- Be praised O God for preserving the peace of my community and country.

- Father, thank you for protecting the borders of my mind, home and community.

- Almighty God, I am grateful, that you do not slumber or sleep and that my life is always in your hands.

- Lord, I celebrate your triumphant doings in my life in the name of Jesus. Amen.

Answers to Prayer

Scriptural Prayer Aids: Psalm 118:5, Ephesians 5:20, Hebrews 13:5
Petition:

- Holy Father, I thank you that you hear me when I pray.

- Lord, I thank you that I can come boldly before your throne and find help in the time of need.

- Most High, I give you praise because when the righteous cry you hear and deliver them.

- Almighty God, I praise you because before I call you will answer and while I am praying you will bring my requests to pass.

- There is no God like you O Lord, who hears your people and answers them speedily.

- Lord, I thank you because I have prayed in faith and because of that, nothing will be withheld from me.

- Lord, you said I should ask and it will be given unto to me, seek and I will find and knock and the door shall be opened to me.

- As I obey your words, let me see the results, today in the name of Jesus.

- Almighty God, you said if I decree a thing it will be established unto me.

- Right now Lord, I decree that the things I desire shall come to me, in very little time, in the name of Jesus.

- Lord, I thank you for disarming the demonic forces which desire to delay the answers to my prayer.

- Father, keep me from anxiety and worry in concerning answers to my prayer.

- Father keep me from frustration and impatience concerning answers to my prayers.

- Lord, because of your faithfulness I will rest in the hope and assurance that you have already accomplished the things I have desired, according to your will, amen.

Nicole McLeary has been a Christian for the past 30 years and has dedicated her life to serving the Christian community and broader society through her areas of giftedness.

As a Minister and Preacher, she connects biblical truths to practical living and challenges believers to enhance their Christian experience. She delivers cutting-edge insights into the word of God and brings the believer on a journey of exploration and greater expression of their rights as kingdom ambassadors. Consequently, she has taught and preached the Word of God in various conferences, seminars, and churches.

She is also an ardent person of prayer and considers it to be one of the most important occupations that God has given to man. As such, one of her major ministerial strengths is engaging the body of Christ in the art of effective prayer. She readily conducts intercessory training sessions and delights in changing the perception of prayer to challenge believers to pursue personal revival and reformation.

As mentor and spiritual leadership coach, she empowers visionaries, leaders, and managers to create sustainable, Christ-centred, prayer-driven visions that put them in the 'driver's seat' of their personal and professional lives so they can maximize their potential.